D0897324

The Executive's Pocket Coach to Diversity and Inclusion Management

A Quick Reference Action Guide

Dr. Edward E. Hubbard, Ph.D.

The Executive's Pocket Coach to Diversity and
Inclusion: A Quick Reference Action Guide

ISBN 978-1-883733-31-5

GLOBAL
INSIGHTS
PUBLISHING

832 Garfield Drive, Petaluma, CA 94954
Office: (707)763-8380   Fax:(435)674-1203

Table of Contents

Contents

Preface

Why should you concern yourself with effective Diversity and Inclusion management? In the past, many managers answered this question out of a sense of the "right thing to do" or because they were seeing more and more people who didn't look like them in the workforce, or merely felt they had to meet the organization's requirement for working with diverse groups. However, today's managers know that without effective diversity management capability, organizational effectiveness is in jeopardy. Being effective at managing a diverse workforce helps to lift morale, improve processes, bring access to new segments of the marketplace, enhance productivity, and improves the financial bottom-line of the organization. In essence, it is good for business.

This Quick Reference Action Guide is designed to help you build Diversity and Inclusion management skills to create a high performing work environment. It should be used as an interactive workbook to test your skills, teach or reinforce diversity concepts and knowledge, and provide tools, processes, and techniques to utilize a diverse workforce to improve organizational performance. Whether you are launching a new diversity initiative, building a diverse work team, or planning a new, innovative product launch, you will find the information in this guidebook an invaluable asset for managerial and leadership development.

The true measure of the effectiveness of this book will be determined in large part by your willingness to read the information, try the exercises, internalize the information, and build on your learning. The first chapter will help you assess your skills in managing diversity and explain its importance to business performance. The next four chapters will help you learn diversity definitions, theories, and concepts that serve as a basic diversity learning foundation. Finally, the remaining chapters provide workplace applications for

key diversity-related initiatives, strategies for building
boosting productivity, approaches for managing the
diversity change process, and building a personal action
plan.

As you read this guide, you will gain awareness,
knowledge, skills, tools, and techniques that will help
you improve your ability to manage diversity. This
guide will help you test your diversity leadership
awareness and knowledge, save management time, help
you navigate difficult situations, provide techniques for
teamwork and improve your interpersonal
effectiveness. In short, it is designed for anyone who
would like to improve their personal diversity
management and leadership performance as well as the
performance of their organization.

Acknowledgements

This book is dedicated to my loving wife Myra. She continues to be my inspiration and source of strength. In addition, no one creates a book like this without the direct or indirect help of many people. They include all of the many scholars quoted and/or used as a resource in this guidebook and many others too numerous to mention. I thank you all. And finally, this book is dedicated to all of the current and future champions of diversity. I hope that it helps you and others realize the truly unlimited potential of a diverse workforce and the importance of your Diversity and Inclusion management contributions!

Chapter One:
Assessing Your Skills

The purpose of this chapter is to provide you with information to help assess your current level of skill in managing Diversity and Inclusion. While you may be anxious to get right to work learning and developing your skills, the best place to start is with an assessment of your current skill level to indicate your starting point.

The Managing Diversity Profile

Before you begin reading this pocket guide, take a minute to complete the Managing Diversity Profile (adapted from the comprehensive 360° Diversity Leadership Competency Profile from Hubbard & Hubbard, Inc.). It is designed to examine your current level of skill for managing diversity and is used as a

self-assessment to give you feedback on six key
competencies for managing diversity.

Managing Diversity Profile by Dr. Edward E.
Hubbard

Directions: This questionnaire is designed to help
you examine your diversity management skills. We
hope you will be frank and honest in answering these
questions, and that you indicate your rating based upon
what you believe to be true about how you respond in a
diverse work environment. You should indicate your
answer by placing a *single* checkmark in the brackets
next to the appropriate term that best reflects "***what you
actually do***" — for example, [✓] Never, or [✓] Rarely,
or [✓] Sometimes, **or** [✓] Often, or [✓] Usually, **or**
[✓] Almost Always. Only **one** checkmark should be
indicated for each question.

Section One

1. I communicate a Diversity and Inclusion vision for organizational success that sparks excitement and enthusiasm in others.

[1] Almost Never

[2] Rarely

[3] Sometimes

[4] Often

[5] Usually

[6] Almost Always

2. I encourage managers to promote and explain our vision for Diversity and Inclusion.

[1] Almost Never

[2] Rarely

[3] Sometimes

[4] Often

[5] Usually

[6] Almost Always

3. I regularly measure the Diversity and Inclusion progress and the progress of our staff towards the diversity and inclusion vision.

[1] Almost Never

[2] Rarely

[3] Sometimes

[4] Often

[5] Usually

[6] Almost Always

4. I ask employees for their input to the Diversity and Inclusion vision.

[1] Almost Never

[2] Rarely

[3] Sometimes

[4] Often

[5] Usually

[6] Almost Always

Section Two

5. I communicate easily with people of diverse backgrounds, races, gender, abilities, or other diverse characteristics.

[1] Almost Never

[2] Rarely

[3] Sometimes

[4] Often

[5] Usually

[6] Almost Always

6. I speak in ways that includes, values, and respects others when expressing my point of view.

[1] Almost Never

[2] Rarely

[3] Sometimes

[4] Often

[5] Usually

[6] Almost Always

7. I give constructive feedback effectively to all groups regardless of race, gender, or other diverse characteristics.

[1] Almost Never

[2] Rarely

[3] Sometimes

[4] Often

[5] Usually

[6] Almost Always

8. I listen to feedback from diverse groups without becoming defensive.

[1] Almost Never

[2] Rarely

[3] Sometimes

[4] Often

[5] Usually

[6] Almost Always

Section Three

9. I discuss Diversity and Inclusion as a strength in our organization.

[1] Almost Never

[2] Rarely

[3] Sometimes

[4] Often

[5] Usually

[6] Almost Always

10. I give people of diverse backgrounds equal opportunity for training, promotion, etc.

[1] Almost Never

[2] Rarely

[3] Sometimes

[4] Often

[5] Usually

[6] Almost Always

11. I seek to understand the cultural norms and practices of groups other than your own.

[1] Almost Never

[2] Rarely

[3] Sometimes

[4] Often

[5] Usually

[6] Almost Always

12. I make use of the diverse talents of people in work assignments, decision-making, etc.

[1] Almost Never

[2] Rarely

[3] Sometimes

[4] Often

[5] Usually

[6] Almost Always

Section Four

13. I consult with diverse groups to find innovative ways to make change happen.

[1] Almost Never

[2] Rarely

[3] Sometimes

[4] Often

[5] Usually

[6] Almost Always

14. I get input from employees about changes that will have an impact on them.

[1] Almost Never

[2] Rarely

[3] Sometimes

[4] Often

[5] Usually

[6] Almost Always

15. I work to resolve diverse work group issues related to impending changes.

[1] Almost Never

[2] Rarely

[3] Sometimes

[4] Often

[5] Usually

[6] Almost Always

16. I keep people informed during the process of change.

[1] Almost Never

[2] Rarely

[3] Sometimes

[4] Often

[5] Usually

[6] Almost Always

Section Five

17. I solicit input from groups regardless of their race, gender, status, or other characteristics.

[1] Almost Never

[2] Rarely

[3] Sometimes

[4] Often

[5] Usually

[6] Almost Always

18. I manage more like a colleague than as a boss.

[1] Almost Never

[2] Rarely

[3] Sometimes

[4] Often

[5] Usually

[6] Almost Always

19. I share accountability with diverse groups equitably.

[1] Almost Never

[2] Rarely

[3] Sometimes

[4] Often

[5] Usually

[6] Almost Always

20. I reward diverse groups for their contributions in a fair manner.

[1] Almost Never

[2] Rarely

[3] Sometimes

[4] Often

[5] Usually

[6] Almost Always

Section Six

21. I delegate responsibility fully to those qualified to do the work regardless of race, gender, or other diverse characteristics.

[1] Almost Never

[2] Rarely

[3] Sometimes

[4] Often

[5] Usually

[6] Almost Always

22. I work to customize training needs to fit diverse work group members.

[1] Almost Never

[2] Rarely

[3] Sometimes

[4] Often

[5] Usually

[6] Almost Always

23. I counsel and mentor diverse work group members on their interests, preferences, and careers.

[1] Almost Never

[2] Rarely

[3] Sometimes

[4] Often

[5] Usually

[6] Almost Always

24. I demonstrate valuing Diversity and Inclusion through my actions.

[1] Almost Never

[2] Rarely

[3] Sometimes

[4] Often

[5] Usually

[6] Almost Always

Scoring Process:

Each question has a possible maximum score of 6 points

Step One: Enter the scores in the *"Profile Scoring Grid"* below using the following numbers for each response (for example, if you placed a checkmark in the brackets next to the term "Usually" then Usually = 5 points:

[**1**] Almost Never

[**2**] Rarely

[**3**] Sometimes

[**4**] Often

[**5**] Usually

[**6**] Almost Always

Step Two: After indicating the numerical points in the left-hand side of the Profile Scoring Grid, add your scores horizontally (across) and draw a "bar" in the appropriate boxes on the right under the *"Total Score*

Graph" based upon the total points (pts) you tallied.
See sample below: (5pts+6pts+2pts+1pts = 14 Points):

Profile Scoring Grid Sample				Total Score Graph							
Questions				Competency	1 to 4	5 to 6	7 to 10	11 to 12	13 to 16	17 to 18	19 to 22	23 to 24
1	2	3	4	Champion for Diversity Max: 24pts Score:								
5	6	2	1									

Profile Scoring Grid Sample				Total Score Graph							
Questions				Competency	1 to 4	5 to 6	7 to 10	11 to 12	13 to 16	17 to 18	19 to 22	23 to 24
1	2	3	4	Champion for Diversity Max: 24pts Score:								
5	6	7	8	Communi-cate Across Cultures Max: 24pts Score:								
9	10	11	12	Diversity Orientation Max: 24pts Score:								
13	14	15	16	Leads Change Max: 24pts Score:								

Profile Scoring Grid Sample				Total Score Graph							
Questions			Competency	1 to 4	5 to 6	7 to 10	11 to 12	13 to 16	17 to 18	19 to 22	23 to 24
17	18	19	20	Empowers Others to Act Max: 24pts Score:							
21	22	23	24	Develops Other Max: 24pts Score:							
				Overall Profile Score Sum of All Competency Totals / 6 Max: 24pts Score:							

Your *Overall Profile Score* is the sum totals of all categories (Champion for Diversity, Communicates Across Cultures, Diversity Orientation, Leads Change, Empowers Others to Act, and Develops Others) **Divided by 6**. Add scores horizontally and draw a "bar" in the appropriate boxes on the right under the *"Total Score Graph"* based upon the total points.

Interpreting Your Score

The interpretation of your *Overall Profile Score* is shown below:

Excellent: (20 to 24)

Congratulations! You have successfully integrated the Diversity and Inclusion management competencies into your style and the way you interact with others. This makes it possible for you and the organization to strategically capitalize on employee differences. You should try to expand your lessons learned as personal

development and help others in your organization that
may not be as far along as you.

Very Good: (17 to 19)

You are making progress and have all the ingredients
for even greater success. Focus on the areas that
received the lower scores and address them.

Average: (15 to 16)

You have some core strengths but there are areas for
growth and improvement. Review the areas that
received the lowest scores and discuss them with your
manager and/or a peer coach/mentor who is effective at
managing a diverse workforce. At the same time, also
look at one or two areas that received the highest scores
and think about ways to sustain these strengths

Poor – Potential Problems Ahead: (14 and
below)

You may already be running into problems managing
your diverse workforce. Pick one or two key
competency areas that received low scores on the
assessment, and focus your efforts using the skills
outlined in this pocket guide. Consider obtaining a peer
coach/mentor who is effective at managing a diverse
workforce to help you bring your skills to a high
performing level. Attend Managing Diversity and
Inclusion workshops and other developmental activities
for improvement.

To get you started, you will find a *"**Managing
Diversity Profile Action Plan Start-up Toolkit"*** packed
with recommended activities, suggestions and tools you
can use to enhance your skills in each area.

MDP - Action Plan Start-up Toolkit

If You Want To Build Skills to...	Actions You Can Take Include...	Resources You Can Use Include...
Become a Champion for Diversity	Make Diversity and Inclusion not just a business strategy, but a way of life. Demonstrate a zero-tolerance policy towards any type of discrimination (age, race, sex, class, sexual orientation, physical ability, etc). Hold managers accountable for communicating and implementing the diversity vision	• Film: Diversity Making It Work: Interview with Dr. Edward E. Hubbard, American Media Films, available from Hubbard & Hubbard, Inc., Petaluma, CA, 1999

If You Want To Build Skills to...	Actions You Can Take Include...	Resources You Can Use Include...
Effectively Communicate Across Cultures	Become aware of your own reaction to change, as well as your ability to interact with others who are different from you, your adaptability to alternative solutions and unstructured situations, your mental flexibility, and your intellectual curiosity. Choose a colleague to meet with regularly who also wishes to manage with more sensitivity to differences. Share goals, set milestones, and report on progress.	▪ Book: Voices of Diversity ▪ Book: Thomas, R. Roosevelt, Building a House for Diversity

If You Want To Build Skills to...	Actions You Can Take Include...	Resources You Can Use Include...
Effectively Communicate Across Cultures	Participate and speak at events in organizations/events where you are different from others in attendance Publicize diversity success stories and show the business relevance. Seek out and build relationships with people who are different than you in race, gender, ethnicity, physical ability, sexual orientation, age, etc.	Book: Communicating in a Diverse Workplace, Kuga, Lillian A. Available through Hubbard & Hubbard, Inc. Book: Fernandez, J, Managing a Diverse Workforce: Regaining the Competitive Edge

If You Want To Build Skills to...	Actions You Can Take Include...	Resources You Can Use Include...
Develop a Diversity Orientation	Learn about differences in the workforce through reading, attending workshops, fostering relationships with people who are different, and participating in activities that are diversity related. Strive to "get it". One of the most frequent statements made by employees talking about diversity in organizations is that some "just don't get it".	Diversity Leadership Competency Profile Film: True Colors, ABC News, Mentor a person who is different in gender, race, ethnicity, physical ability, etc. Learn about various types of mentoring: formal, informal, or facilitated. Coronet/MTI Films

If You Want To Build Skills to...	Actions You Can Take Include...	Resources You Can Use Include...
Develop a Diversity Orientation	They hear others not believing that some employees may be treated differently. If you think you may not get it, pursue additional education. Ask questions of people who are different from you. Ask them what it is you don't get. Listen to others as they describe diversity issues. Seek clarification, rather than making hasty judgments.	Film: Homophobia in the Workplace, Training Express, Des Moines, IA Film: The Color of Fear, Lee Mun Wah, Stir Fry Productions, Oakland, CA

If You Want To Build Skills to...	Actions You Can Take Include...	Resources You Can Use Include...
Lead Change	Offer to coordinate or participate in an event that educates others about a specific diversity topic or view. Volunteer for a tough diversity assignment in your workplace or community to help find solutions to meet the needs of a diverse population. Be proactive in looking for chances to stretch yourself and learn something. Begin a staff meeting with the following question: "What actions did you take last week to utilize the strength of our diversity to make our performance even better this week?" Persist in asking this question for at least three meetings in a row so that everyone knows you're serious about diversity and its importance for performance and change.	Measuring Diversity Results by Dr. Edward E. Hubbard, available through Hubbard & Hubbard, Inc. Harvard Business Review on Managing Diversity, Harvard Business School Press, 2001.

If You Want To Build Skills to...	Actions You Can Take Include...	Resources You Can Use Include...
	By the way, bo prepared to answer this same question for yourself at each meeting. Get involved in recruiting efforts in your department. Help develop strategies for increasing the number of women, people of color, people of different ages, persons with disabilities, and those whose lifestyles differ from the traditional employee background. Develop concrete performance measurement criteria to evaluate all managers' efforts in managing a diverse workforce. Set up rewards for those who do well in these areas and penalties for those who do poorly.	Book: Thomas, R. Roosevelt, Building a House for Diversity available through Hubbard & Hubbard, Inc. 707-763-8380

If You Want To Build Skills to...	Actions You Can Take Include...	Resources You Can Use Include...
	Make certain that all training programs and systems relating to managerial/supervisory skill development have modules that deal with aspects of diversity and its importance to the business of the organization.	

If You Want To Build Skills to...	Actions You Can Take Include...	Resources You Can Use Include...
Empower Others to Act	Find ways to increase interactions among people who need to work more effectively together. Teamwork and trust can only be built when people interact informally as well as formally. Establish easily accessible, common meeting areas that encourage people to interact.	Book: Simons, G, Working Together: How to Become More Effective in a Multicultural Environment Team Building for Diverse Work Groups, Myers, Selma G. available through Hubbard & Hubbard, Inc. 707-763-8380

If You Want To Build Skills to...	Actions You Can Take Include...	Resources You Can Use Include...
	Put the coffee pot or the popcorn maker in a location between groups that should talk to each other.	
	Ask other people from other parts of the organization to attend your regular staff meetings.	
	Schedule a lunch for two or more groups that don't spend much time face to face.	

If You Want To Build Skills to...	Actions You Can Take Include...	Resources You Can Use Include...
Develop Others	Develop effective listening and delegation skills. Integrate diversity into your business plan. Review development plan (IDPs) actions for completeness, talent utilization, and provide required support. Create a random spot check procedure to examine Individual Development Plans (IDPs) for women, people of color, and any other underrepresented group	▪ Managing Work Expectations Profile – A self-assessment, self-scoring instrument. Inscape Products, distributed by Hubbard & Hubbard, Inc. 707-763-8380 ▪ 101 Actions You Can Take To Value and Manage Diversity by Julie O'Mara available from Hubbard & Hubbard, Inc. ▪ Book: Tannen, Deborah, Talking 9 to 5: Women and Men in the Workplace

If You Want To Build Skills to...	Actions You Can Take Include...	Resources You Can Use Include...
	Inventory your employees' educational background, work experiences, job knowledge, specialized skills, number of opportunities they have had to gain development, participate in special skill building assignments, the amount of cross-training they have received, etc.	

If You Want To Build Skills to...	Actions You Can Take Include...	Resources You Can Use Include...
	Train managers and direct reports in effective career planning, development and coaching skills when working with others who are different from you.

Spend time identifying their specific roles and responsibilities and how you will measure their progress | |

Managing and leading in a diverse work environment, in general, requires that you follow these ten guidelines:

Ten Guidelines for Managing and Leading in a Diverse Work Environment*	
☑	**Activity**
	Search out challenging opportunities to utilize diversity to change, grow, innovate, and improve.
	Experiment, take risks, learn from the accompanying mistakes, and seek feedback.
	Envision an inclusive, strategically anchored future using diversity.
	Enlist others in a common vision by incorporating and appealing to their values, interests, hopes, and dreams.
	Foster collaboration by promoting cooperative goal setting and building trust.

Ten Guidelines for Managing and Leading in a Diverse Work Environment*	
☑	**Activity**
	Strengthen people by giving power away, providing choices, developing competence, assigning critical tasks, and offering visible support.
	Set the example by seeking cultural knowledge and behaving in ways that are consistent with shared values.
	Achieve small wins that promote consistent progress and build commitment by sharing measurable diversity results.

☑	Ten Guidelines for Managing and Leading in a Diverse Work Environment*
	Activity
	Recognize individual contributions to the success of every project in the manner consistent with the contributor's needs and wants.
	Celebrate diverse work team accomplishments regularly.

* Adapted from James M. Kouzes and Barry Z Posner's "Ten Commandments of Leadership

Building Diversity Management Capability

Why should you concern yourself with effective diversity and inclusion management? In the past, many managers answered this question out of a sense of the "right thing to do" or because they were seeing more and more people who didn't look like them in the workforce, or merely felt they had to meet the organization's requirement for working with diverse groups. However, today's managers know that without effective diversity management capability, organizational effectiveness is in jeopardy. Being effective at managing a diverse workforce helps to lift morale, improve processes, bring access to new segments of the marketplace and enhance productivity of the organization. In essence, it is good for business.

In profit-making organizations, maximizing the difference between revenues and costs optimizes performance. This same goal exists in many non-profit organizations, except that the result is called surplus instead of profits. The question therefore is: "How is workforce diversity and its management related to revenues, costs, or both?" To answer this question we can explore several concepts and strategies that illustrate the impact of diversity on business performance. These concepts and strategies include items such as marketing strategies, problem-solving strategies, creativity and innovation that can be viewed as important factors in revenue generation.

Marketing Strategies

We live in an increasing global world that is diverse. Whether your business includes marketing financial services, computers, telecommunications products, social services, health care equipment, manufacturing processes, engineering expertise, and the like, expertise in addressing a diverse customer market will be essential to your success. For example, an automobile manufacturer in Japan cannot afford to ignore the fact that nearly half of all new car buyers in the United States are women. This is true regardless of the gender make up of car buyers in Japan. Likewise, no reasonable person in the consumer-goods industry can afford to ignore the fact that roughly a quarter of the world's population is Chinese and immigration to the United States from mostly Asian and Latin American countries is occurring at a rate of more than a million people per year.

The buying power of minority groups in the U.S. has reached new heights and continues to outpace cumulative inflation, according to the Multicultural Economy Report from the Selig Center for Economic Growth at the University of Georgia Terry College of Business.

For example, at $1.3 trillion, the 2014 Hispanic market was larger than the economy of all but 15 countries in the world

The report breaks down the economy by racial and ethnic affiliation, supplying buying power estimates for African Americans, Asians, Native Americans and Hispanics. It also includes state-by-state buying power projections, providing businesses with a blueprint for market growth across the U.S.

The term "buying power" refers to the total personal income of residents that is available after taxes. It does not included dollars that are borrowed or were previously saved.

As these groups increase in number and purchasing power, their growing shares of the U.S. consumer market draw avid attention from producers, retailers, and service providers alike.

The buying power data presented here and differences in spending by race and/or ethnicity suggest that one general advertisement, product, or service geared for all consumers increasingly miss many potentially profitable market opportunities. As the U.S. consumer market becomes more diverse, advertising, products, and media must be tailored to each market segment.

With this in mind, new entrepreneurs, established businesses, marketing specialists, economic development organizations, and chambers of commerce now seek estimates of the buying power of the nation's major racial and ethnic minority groups.

Buying Power Statistics by Race

African Americans

Black buying power was estimated to rise to $1.1 trillion in 2014. African Americans control the second biggest minority market, behind Hispanics. Black buying power has seen an 86 percent increase since 2000 and accounts for 8.7 percent of the nation's total. The growth in black buying power stems in part from an increase in the number of black-owned businesses as well as from an uptick in education among the African-American population, which leads to higher incomes.

Native Americans

The Native population will see their buying power increase 149 percent since 2000, to $100 billion. That increase is larger than the percentage growth in the white population, and is due in part to rapid growth of the Native American population.

Although Natives comprise only 1.3 percent of the total U.S. population, their buying power and clustered populations should make them especially attractive to businesses.

Asians

The Selig Center estimated that Asian buying power will rise to $770 billion in 2014, with 5.5 percent of the U.S. population claiming Asian ancestry. (This number includes those who identified as Asian as well as Native Hawaiian or Other Pacific Islander.)

Despite the Great Recession, employment gains for Asians grew 45 percent since 2000. Those strong gains coupled with a fast-growing immigrant population mean that Asian buying power is expected to grow to $1 trillion in 2019.

Hispanics

One of out every six people in the U.S. claims Hispanic origin, making the group an economic powerhouse. The $1.3 trillion 2014 Hispanic market shows a gain of 155 percent since 2000, which is far greater gain than the 71 percent increase in non-

Hispanic buying power and the 76 percent increase in overall buying power since that time.

The Selig Center estimates that by 2019 Hispanics will account for 10.6 percent of total U.S. buying power.

To be effective managers in organizations must possess effective multicultural marketing savvy to meet specific needs of a diverse marketplace to affect buying behavior.

If an organization plans to sell or deliver goods and services in a diverse marketplace, it must be fully capable of effectively utilizing its diverse workforce in key strategic ways. For instance, it is important from a public relations point of view to be viewed as a company that is known for managing and utilizing its diverse workforce assets well. There are a number of well-publicized ratings for "The Best Company for Working Women and Working Mothers", "The Most

Admired Company" and the "The Top 50 Companies for Women and Minorities". This fuels a public relations climate where workforce talent and consumers make choices about the organizations they would work for and buy from. This line of thinking is also supported by a study of stock price responses to publicity that changed either positively or negatively on an organization's ability to manage diversity. The authors found that announcements of awards for exemplary efforts resulted in significant positive changes in stock prices while announcements of discrimination suits resulted in significant negative changes in stock prices (Wright, Ferris, Hiller & Kroll, 1995).

In addition, organizations can gain a lot from the insights of its diverse workforce to understand the cultural effects of buying decisions and mapping strategies to respond to them. Depending on the product or service delivered by the organization, many employees may also represent part of the firm's customer base! A good reputation inside the organization can help product and service sales outside the organization. Another key marketing strategy includes tapping employee network or resource groups. They can be an excellent resource for focus groups, feedback and ideas for honing the organization's reach into diverse marketplace opportunities.

Problem Solving

Revenue increases can also show up due to improvements in diverse work team problem solving and decision-making. Diverse work teams have a broader and richer base of experience to draw on in solving organizations problems and issues. The presence of minority views creates higher levels of critical analysis of assumptions and implications of decisions. In addition, it also generates an increase in the number of alternatives from which the group chooses. Problem solving benefits from diverse work groups do not happen by simply mixing people together who are culturally different. The improved outcomes heavily depend on a diversity-competent manager utilizing key diversity management behaviors.

In one study, researchers found that properly managed and trained diverse work teams produced scores that were six times higher than homogeneous teams. Researchers also found that it is important how a diverse team uses its diversity. For example, those diverse teams that recognized and utilized their diversity had higher productivity. Even when the team was diverse, if that diversity is not used effectively, it can cause process problems that result in lower team productivity. The essential variable is the ability to "*effectively manage and utilize the team's diversity*".

Creativity and Innovation

Creativity and innovation can be vital to an organization's ability to perform. New product introductions, advertising, process re-engineering, quality improvements and the like are examples where these skills are required. Diverse work teams have also been found to promote improved creativity and innovation that generates revenue. In her book The Change Masters (1983), Rosabeth Moss Kanter notes that highly innovative companies have done a better job of eradicating racism, sexism, and classism; tend to have workforces that are more race and gender diverse, and take deliberate steps to create heterogeneous work teams with the objective of bringing that diversity to bear on organizational problems and issues.

As you read this guide, you will gain awareness, knowledge, skills, tools and techniques that will help you improve your ability to manage diversity. This guide will help you test your awareness and knowledge, save time, facilitate difficult situations, provide techniques for teamwork and improve your interpersonal effectiveness. Now that you have had an opportunity to assess your skills, you are ready to gain a better understanding of requirements for managing diversity. Often the best place to start is with a

definition of diversity, which we will explore, in the
next chapter.

References

Hubbard, Edward E., "Diversity Leadership
Competency Profile, Global Insights Publishing,
Petaluma, CA, 2001.

Hubbard, Edward E., "Managing Diversity Profile,
Global Insights Publishing, Petaluma, CA, 1999, 2003.

Hubbard, Edward E., "Techniques for Managing a
Diverse Workforce", Global Insights Publishing,
Petaluma, CA, 2002.

Humphreys, Jeff, Director of the Selig Center
Multicultural Economy Report, The Selig Center for
Economic Growth at the University of Georgia Terry
College of Business, Atlanta, GA, 2014.

Kouzes, James M, Posner, Barry Z., "Leadership
Practices Inventory", Jossey-Bass, Pfeiffer, San
Francisco, CA, 2001.

Moss Kanter, Rosabeth, "The Change Masters"
Simon & Schuster, New York, 1983

"101 Actions You Can Take To Value and Manage
Diversity" by Julie O'Mara, O'Mara & Associates,
Castro Valley, CA, 1999

Chapter Two: What is Diversity? What is Inclusion?

Definition and Terms

Any useful discussion of the topic of diversity must start with a fundamental clarification of the term. The term *diversity* itself has a number of different interpretations. *"Diversity"* can be defined as a **"collective mixture characterized by differences and similarities that are applied in pursuit of organizational objectives"**. *"Diversity Management"* then can be defined as *"the process of planning for, organizing, directing, and supporting these collective mixtures in a way that adds a measurable difference to organizational performance"*.

Diversity and its mixtures can be organized into four interdependent and sometimes overlapping aspects: Workforce Diversity, Behavioral Diversity, Structural Diversity, and Business Diversity.

Workforce Diversity encompasses group and situational identities of the organization's employees (i.e., gender, race, ethnicity, religion, sexual orientation, physical ability, age, family status, economic background and status, and geographical background and status). It also includes changes in the labor market demographics.

Behavioral Diversity encompasses work styles, thinking styles, learning styles, communication styles, aspirations, beliefs/value system as well as changes in the attitudes and expectation on the part of employees.

Structural Diversity encompasses interactions across functions, across organizational levels in the hierarchy, across divisions and between parent

companies and subsidiaries, across organizations
engaged in strategic alliances and cooperative ventures.
As organizations attempt to become more flexible, less
layered, more team-based, and more multi- and cross-
functional, measuring this type of diversity will require
more attention.

Business Diversity encompasses the expansion and
segmentation of customer markets, the diversification
of products and services offered, and the variety of
operating environments in which organizations work
and compete (i.e., legal and regulatory context, labor
market realities, community and societal
expectations/relationships, business cultures and
norms). Increasing competitive pressures, globalization,
rapid advances in product technologies, changing
demographics in the customer bases both within
domestic markets and across borders, and shifts in
business/government relationships all signal a need to
measure an organization's response and impact on
business diversity.

Inclusion is the invisible thread that ties the elements of an organization's culture together. It helps to promote open communication, knowledge sharing and innovation by creating a collegial, mutually respectful environment. It allows workers to bring their full capabilities to bear in the workplace by fostering a unified culture of acceptance and idea utilization.

I define "inclusiveness" as the act or process of using the information, tools, skills, insights, and other talents that each individual has to offer that results in the measurable, mutual benefit and gain of everyone. It also includes providing everyone with opportunities to contribute their thoughts, ideas, and concerns. If present, inclusiveness results in people feeling valued and respected. When applied effectively, "Inclusiveness" results in increased engagement, improved product, service delivery, and enhanced financial performance.

As you can see, diversity and inclusion are a mosaic of mixtures that includes everyone, representing their differences and similarities, and the variety of processes, systems, and aspects of the global environment in which the organization must respond. An organization's inherent bias about diversity can cloud the definition and is often reflected in the way it is positioned and defined by executives and managers. When executives and managers have not internalized the important message that diversity includes everyone, their comments frequently imply that "white males need not apply." In many organizations, diversity has been positioned to focus on women and people of color therefore a "diverse person" in such an organization cannot be a white man.

Some organizations use diversity as a shorthand for a variety of characteristics such as learning style, individual thinking style, and so on, but often leave out issues of differences involving race, gender, age, physical abilities and sexual orientation. In any event,

the definitions are less comprehensive than they should
be to address the real opportunities and complex issues
that diversity offers. Given today's workplace and
marketplace challenges, with fierce competition for
talent and market share, market pressures for
responsiveness, etc., diversity and inclusion offers
many opportunities and advantages. The entire
organization must clearly understand what diversity and
inclusion management truly means and realizes that
diversity and inclusion involves everyone.

Primary and Secondary Dimensions

A fundamental error that some people make is to
view diversity as synonymous with the word "culture."
They diversity is focused on "what Hispanics do in
their culture" or "what women want." This approach is
inherently flawed because it reinforces stereotypes,
which those who truly value diversity are trying to
eliminate.

People come in a variety of shapes, sizes and colors. This variety helps differentiate us. While we share the important dimensions of humanness with all members of our species, there are biological and environmental differences separate and distinguish us as individuals and groups. It is this vast array of physical and cultural differences that constitute the spectrum of human diversity.

Since we are different, our definition of diversity must include important human characteristics that impact an individual's values, opportunities, and perceptions of themselves and others at work and by highlighting how individuals aggregate into larger subgroups based upon shared characteristics. Using these criteria, a workplace definition would, at bare minimum, include:

- Age
- Ethnicity
- Gender

- Mental/physical abilities and characteristics
- Race
- Sexual orientation

These six differences are called "*core*" or "*primary*" dimensions of diversity because they exert and important impact on our early socialization and a powerful, sustained impact throughout every stage of life. These six dimensions represent properties and characteristics that constitute the core of our diverse identities. All individuals have a variety of dimensions of diversity through which they experience the world and by which they are defined. At the core of each of us, there is at least a minimum of these six dimensions.

Beyond the six *primary* dimensions, there are several "secondary" dimensions that play an important role in shaping our values, expectations, and experiences as well. These include:

- Communication style

- Education
- Family status
- Military experience
- Organizational role and level
- Religion
- First language
- Geographic location
- Income
- Work experience
- Work style

Like the core dimensions, these secondary
dimensions share certain characteristics. Generally,
they are more variable in nature, less visible to others
around us, and more variable in the degree of influence
they exert on our individual lives. Many secondary
dimensions contain an element of control or choice.
Because we acquire, discard, and modify these
dimensions, their power is less constant and more
individualized than is true for the core dimensions. Yet
despite the fact that these dimensions have less life-long

influence, most individuals are more conscious of their impact at a given point in time than they are regarding primary dimensions. Usually, it is easier to see the connection of these secondary dimensions and events in someone's life (e.g., their first language might influence their communications style, their education level might influence their organizational role and level, etc.)

Often people refer to primary dimensions as those they are able to see. They include things people know about us before we open our mouths, because they are physically visible (except sexual orientation). When people feel they are being stereotyped based upon primary dimensions, they can become sensitive about it. People are usually less sensitive about secondary dimensions; because they are elements we have made a choice on or have the power to change. We also have the choice of whether to disclose the information or not; we can conceal it if we like.

Think about which dimensions have the most impact on you as a person. The primary dimensions are important, nonetheless, we are greatly influenced by where we live, whether we are married or not, and our financial status. The primary and secondary dimensions help us perceive each other's uniqueness far beyond our culture or communications style. They really help us begin to define who we really are as unique individuals.

An example of these Primary and Secondary Dimensions of Diversity is shown below:

Primary and Secondary Dimensions of Diversity Model

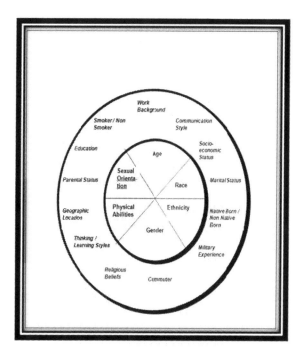

From Loden and Rosner

One of the major areas of difficulty in dealing with
diversity is how people react to difference. In most
cases, peoples' responses have already been imprinted
since early childhood, based upon a wide range of
influences. When individuals start to realize the extent
to which these influences have shaped their perceptions,
awareness begins. Awareness then leads to greater
understanding and ultimately, the potential to build a
positive environment. Awareness also opens a window
of opportunity for you and the organization to focus on
a new, more effective path. The challenge for you as a
manager of today's workplace is to harness the strength
of this diversity, to nurture it and mold it into the
productive workplace the organization needs and
desires.

A diverse workplace is inevitable, but the benefits
of diversity are not unless that diversity is utilized in a
way that adds a measurable difference to organizational
performance. The environment within the organization
will determine if the benefits of diversity are realized.

Specific steps must be taken to create an environment where all employees feel welcome, valued for what they bring to the organization and their talents utilized. While each diversity dimension adds a layer of complexity, it is the dynamic interaction among all dimensions of diversity that influences a person's self-image, values, opportunities, and expectations. And, from an organizational standpoint, offers a tremendous opportunity for improved performance and competitive advantage.

Diversity Statistics Quiz

The statistical demographics of today's workplace will change from region to region, and occupation to occupation. The only constant is that we continue to develop and change through the individual contributions of a vast combination of cultures, languages and abilities all working together to achieve

success. This requires that managers are aware and
sensitive to differences in the workplace and us that
knowledge without reinforcing negative stereotypes.
What's your level of knowledge of diversity? The quiz
below will help you gain information regarding changes
related to diversity and explore the possible
implications and impact on your organization. Simply
complete the worksheet below. Answers to the quiz can
be found at the end of the chapter.

Diversity Quiz

1. By the year 2020, what will be the estimated
    percentage of females in the
    workforce?_____%

2. Of the 8.7 million immigrants who arrived in
    the U.S. between 1980 and 1990, what percent
    have college degrees? What percentage of U.S.

natives has college degrees?_____%
_____%

3. In the U.S., what percent of male executives
under age 40 are fathers? What percent of
female executives under age 40 are mothers?
____% ____%

4. What are the two most racially and ethnically
diverse states in the U.S.? The two least?
_____?
_____?

5. How many people indicated they were "multi-
racial" in the 2010 Census? Select a letter: a)
1 Million b) 20 Million c) 12 Million d)
9 Million

6. Women make up _____ percent of all
shoppers in the US; they spend ____ cents of
every dollar. (fill in the blanks)

7. By the year 2050, what percent of the total
   United States population will Asians,
   Hispanics, Blacks, and other nonwhite groups
   represent?

8. What demographic group represents the fastest
   growing customer base in the United States?

9. What are the top six frequently cited barriers
   to advancement listed by women in the
   workplace?

10. One out of _____ black households makes
    more than $50,000 per year?

Interpreting Your Answers

As you review your answers to this diversity quiz,
ask yourself the following questions:

- What questions were the most difficult? Why?
- Which of your answers were the most surprising? Why?
- Which demographics will potentially have the most impact on your organization? Why
- What are the most significant implications of these changing demographics?

Workplace Trends

There are a number of studies that have followed the changing mosaic of America. One of the most widely publicized studies was commissioned by the U.S. Department of Labor and Conducted by the Hudson Institute. They have completed two studies: "*Workforce 2000*" in 1987, and ten years later "*Workforce 2020*" in 1997. The most significant trends in the U.S. population are:

- Decreasing percentage of Caucasians
- Increasing percentage of people of color
- Decreasing birth rates
- Increasing percentages of people in their middle and older years

These trends translate into significant changes in the workforce composition, from more homogeneous to heterogeneous:

| Changing Trend from a Homogeneous Workforce to a More Heterogeneous Workforce ||
Homogeneous	Heterogeneous
• White Male	• Women & Minorities
• 29 Years Old	• 40+ Years Old
• Married with Children	• Variety of Lifestyles
• Less than 12 Years Education	• 12+ Years of Education

Because of these changes in the workforce,
organizations must be prepared to deal with:

- An equal balance of men and women
- Shrinking numbers of whites and increasing
  numbers of people of color
- Most *new entrants* to the workforce will be
  women or people of color (over 85 percent in
  the 21st Century)
- A shortage of *new entrants* in the workforce
  under age 24
- An increasing percentage of people aged 35 to
  55 and older

Compared with the labor force of the past decades,
today's labor force is older, more racially and ethnically
diverse, and composed of more women. These trends
are expected to continue to shape the future of the
workforce; however, the U.S. labor force is expected to
grow at a slightly slower rate than in previous decades.

The annual growth rate of the U.S. labor force over the 2010–2020 periods is projected to be 0.7 percent, lower than the 0.8-percent growth rate exhibited in the previous decade. The labor force is projected to increase by 10.5 million in the next decade, reaching 164.4 million in 2020.

The slower growth of the labor force is primarily the result of a slower rate of growth in the U.S. population and a noticeable decrease in the labor force participation rate. The civilian non-institutional population 16 years and older had an annual growth rate of 1.1 percent from 2000 to 2010, but is projected to grow by a lesser 1.0 percent during 2010–2020.

The labor force growth over the next few years will be affected by the aging of the baby-boom generation, persons born between 1946 and 1964. The baby boomers will be between the ages of 56 and 74 in 2020, placing them in the 55-years-and-older age group in the labor force, with distinctively lower participation rates than those of the prime age group of 25-to-54-year-olds.

A more diverse population. Immigration has a major role in the growth and makeup of the racial and ethnic composition of the U.S. resident population. Every race and ethnicity is projected to grow over the 2010–2020 period. However, the *share* of White non-Hispanics in the total resident population is expected to decrease.

Minorities' growing shares of that population have been an ongoing trend in the past several decades and are reflected in the Census Bureau and BLS projections of the U.S. population and labor force. Asians and Hispanics are projected to continue to grow much faster than White non-Hispanics.

The rate of growth of the Hispanic population is expected to be the highest of all racial and ethnic groups.

The civilian non-institutional population of Hispanics was 15.9 million in 1990 and 23.9 million in 2000. From 2000 to 2010, their number increased by nearly 10 million, reaching 33.7 million in the latter year. BLS projects that the group will increase by another 12.4 million, to reach more than 46 million in 2020. The Hispanic share of the total civilian non-institutional population will have increased from 11.3 percent in 2000 to 17.5 percent in 2020. Hispanic immigrants to the United States are mostly in younger age groups, and their entry into the country lowers the median age of the working-age population. The high fertility rate of Hispanics offsets the slow growth of the native-born population and increases the overall U.S. fertility rate.

BLS also projects that the Asian population will grow by 2.9 percent between 2010 and 2020 and increase the Asian share of the total civilian non-institutional population to 5.7 percent. In contrast, the share of White non-Hispanics is projected to decline

over the same period. The White non-Hispanic share of
the total civilian non-institutional population was 77.5
percent in 1990, declined to 72.2 percent in 2000, and
fell to a low of 67.6 percent in 2010. The group's share
is projected to decrease further, to 62.7 percent in 2020.

The bottom line is that the workplace of the past no
longer exists and hasn't for quite some time. It is not
like past years when the typical workplace was made up
of a homogeneous group of married white men, who
were 29 years old, married, with less than 12 years of
education. During that time, most of them had wives
who were "stay at home" mothers to care for the
children. Compared to today's reality of a workplace
rich with diverse people from all walks of life,
backgrounds, values, and ways of perceiving the world.
Nonetheless, many organizations are structured for
operation around the "old homogeneous model" that
diminishes their ability to grow and ultimately compete
in a global marketplace.

People in the homogeneous workplace naturally created an American work environment that worked for people present in the workforce at that time with similar backgrounds. When the organizational structure reflected their needs, backgrounds and values, the system worked well for getting things accomplished for those who were in it. It makes little if any sense to blame those who created a system that supported and worked for the workplace needs of the time period. However, as the landscape of America changed, along with its workforce pools and composition, organizations fell woefully behind. Few organizations reflect the needs, backgrounds and values of a diverse America and do not accommodate today's workforce in a way that effectively addresses its requirements for performance.

As far back as 1992, 52 percent of working adults were women, and 11 percent of the men were minorities, which means only 37 percent of working adults were white males- and the percentages are decreasing. It just makes good business sense to

reexamine a situation in which 63 percent of the
workforce may be less productive than they could be
because they work in an outdated system!

With ever-increasing amounts of change in the
workforce, workplace diversity can't be ignored. It's a
critical challenge that must be faced. The first part of
addressing the current trend of a multicultural, diverse
workforce lies in knowing how diversity can impact
your organization. It has both potential downsides and
potential opportunities.

Potential Risks If Diversity and Inclusion Is Not Managed

Workplace diversity can impact an organization in
many ways. For example, if it is not managed properly,
diversity can:

- **Hinder Productivity**, i.e., when diverse work teams are not trained to leverage their uniqueness they bring while avoiding the barriers such as prejudice and stereotypes

- **Create Conflicts**, i.e., effectively managing generational conflicts between younger and more senior workers.

- **Lead to Communication Gaps**, i.e., words, phrases and behavior have different contextual meanings in different cultures, which can lead to misunderstandings and failure.

- **Results in Unfair Hiring/Promotional Preferences**, i.e., during selection interviewing practices of hiring to individual preferences versus real job requirements can develop. Candidates who are qualified based upon the real job requirements may be overlooked, dismissed, or not even selected for interview if these practices are not challenged.

Other workplace changes such as flattened organizations, the need for faster cycle times, team-based or matrix organizational structures can prove challenging to those with an "old-school" model of how organizations used to work in the "homogeneous past". It can also be daunting to new entrants to the workforce who are not prepared to handle this new way of operating, especially if they are put in charge of a group who was familiar and used to the old way.

There are some potential obstacles that must be overcome if an organization is to be successful. Some of them include the following:

- **Societal Traditions** – For example, certain occupations are sometimes associated with certain types of people. In many societies, nurturing roles of secretary, nurse, social workers, and the like are filled primarily filled by women. Older workers and women are often excluded from physical jobs; those

physically or mentally challenged have
difficulty finding work. Those who "buck the
system" and obtain jobs in fields that have
traditionally been held by others or a person of
the opposite sex, typically encounter
resistance.

- **Industry Norms** – Certain industries have
  norms that make it difficult for diverse
  individuals. For example, those in
  construction-related fields or the automotive
  industry often attend trade shows and
  conferences that are male dominated and
  include seductively dressed female spokes
  models. Women or individuals from different
  ethnic groups might feel uncomfortable
  participating or being in those environments.

- **Lack of Awareness** – Many people may not
  be aware or "down-play" the impact of
  diversity on a work environment. They may
  not realize the impact on productivity, morale,
  competitiveness, etc. Only after their

awareness has been raised can an organization
be fully capable of achieving top level
performance.

- **Stereotyping** – Everyone stereotypes.
  Stereotypes are defined as fixed, inflexible
  notions about a group. Stereotypes, whether
  positive or negative, are the heart of prejudice,
  and they block the ability to think about people
  as individuals. Many stereotypical
  generalizations are based upon misconceptions
  and errors in judgment. Sometimes people
  generalize too much or stereotype simply
  because they do not have all facts, have
  limited personal experience, or are utilizing
  distorted information that itself is based on
  stereotypes. In order to take advantage of
  diversity's potential, individuals first must
  learn to identify the stereotypical perceptions
  they hold, and then work toward changing
  them.

Potential Opportunities If Diversity Is Managed Effectively

Workplace diversity can be a tremendous strength and a real ace in the hand of an organization that utilizes these workforce assets strategically. Capitalizing on workplace diversity can help an organization

- **Gain a Competitive Advantage**, i.e., coming up with improved ways and perspectives for doing things faster, cheaper, and better that may be as unique as the diversity of the group which can translate into a unique competitive advantage.
- **Enter New Markets**, i.e., customers from different demographic groups, backgrounds, and countries.

- **Becoming More Creative and Innovative**, i.e., as stated earlier, adding more and different input if these sharing behaviors are cultivated and utilized.
- **Increase Employee Satisfaction**, i.e., when employees don't understand one another, they become frustrated easily. Capitalizing on workplace diversity means learning how to accept differences and working well with others. This helps to increase morale and satisfaction.

Diversity History and Approaches

Diversity History

To understand diversity from a contemporary perspective, it is helpful to briefly review the history of diversity in the U.S. workplace over the last 30 years.

Several governmental initiatives have been enacted with regard to diversity. They include initiatives such as:

Civil Rights Act – This act was created as an outgrowth of the human rights movement and was enacted in 1964. It was the beginning of a wave of social change that continues even today.

Affirmative Action – Shortly after the Civil Rights Act of 1964, Affirmative Action legislation was enacted. Its intent was to ensure that employers took positive steps to attract, promote and retain women and minorities if they were underrepresented in the organization's workforce. This legislation was forced onto employers, and came to be viewed as "quota-filling", which sometimes created animosity between groups. While affirmative action was not the final solution, it was a necessary step appropriate for the times America faced.

Equal Employment Opportunity – Next, Equal Employment Opportunity legislation was enacted to prohibit discrimination on the basis of race, color, religion, sex, national origin, age, disability, or veteran status. It has been updated to include discrimination based upon sexual orientation. EEO attempted to provide applicants and employees with equitable treatment in an organization's human resources and management practices, including recruitment, hiring, training, compensation, and promotion. The Equal Employment Opportunity Commission (EEOC) is now responsible for monitoring and enforcing legislation regarding workplace diversity.

Sexual Harassment – This area became a focus of business in the 1980s and 90s. As more women entered the workforce, incidents of sexual intimidation on the job increased. Research has shown that a large percentage of women report having experienced some sort of sexual harassment. With recent publicity in this area, the courts are making awards on an increasing number of claims.

Americans with Disabilities Act – The most recent human rights legislation was the passing of the Americans with Disabilities Act (ADA) in 1989, which applies to 53 million Americans. ADA requires employers make "reasonable accommodations" in employing people with job-related limitations. The main impact is on selection and job descriptions in employment, and in modifying facilities for buildings and retail outlets. The law includes people with HIV and AIDS, as well as many older people.

Approaches to Diversity

Throughout the years, there have been a number of approaches to manage diversity. Here are a few examples:

The Golden Rule – This approach suggested that we "treat each other like we would like to be treated." However, the majority culture assumed that this meant treating people according to the traditional standards already established. This approach left no room to acknowledge individual differences. This leaves a lot to be desired and does not effectively meet the needs of a diverse workforce.

Right the Wrongs – This approach is often likened to Affirmative Action. It acknowledges that minorities and women have been effectively mistreated when it comes to fair representation in organizations. It often generated a white male backlash and charges of reversed discrimination since some white males and others felt this was nothing but quotas to hire unqualified people and a means to take their jobs away. Dr. Roosevelt Thomas, author of "Beyond Race and Gender", wrote in a 1990 Harvard Business Review article "What managers fear from diversity is lowering of standards, a sense that 'anything goes'. Of course standards must not suffer. In fact, competence counts more than ever. The goal is to manage diversity in such a way as to get from a diverse workforce the same productivity that we once got from a homogeneous workforce. The diversity I'm talking about is not only race, gender, creed, and ethnicity, but also age, background, education, function and personality differences. The objective is not to assimilate minorities and women into the dominant white male culture, but to create a dominant heterogeneous culture." The "right the wrongs" approach created an "us versus them" mentality, which destroys teamwork, productivity, and negatively impacts people and the bottom-line.

Valuing Differences – The "Valuing Differences" approach is inclusive. It acknowledges differences and recognizes that they exist, but the approach doesn't require that people are assimilated into the dominant culture. It incorporates much of the current thinking related to diversity that focuses on diversity as a business imperative and asset.

By using a "Valuing Diversity" approach, diversity becomes equally valuable to traditional employees, because it gives them the freedom to break out of the stereotypes they have been forced to conform to. For diversity to work, organizations must make certain that diversity is viewed as an asset to be utilized to meet its strategic business objectives.

Diversity Statistics Quiz Answers

1. By the year 2020, what will be the estimated percentage of females in the workforce? **Answer:** 50% according to the Hudson Institutes' Workforce 2020 report by Richard W. Judy and Carol D'Amico.

2. Of the 8.7 million immigrants who arrived in the U.S. between 1980 and 1990, what percent have college degrees? What percentage of U.S. natives has college degrees? **Answer:** 23.7% ; 20.3% respectively according to "Perspectives", by Diane Fililowski. Personnel Journal, February 1993.

3. In the U.S., what percent of male executives under age 40 are fathers? What percent of female executives under age 40 are mothers?
    Answer: 90% ; 35% respectively according to "Careers Under Glass", by Charlene Marmer Solomon. Personnel Journal, April 1990, p. 102.

4. What are the two most racially and ethnically diverse states in the U.S.? The two least?
    Answer: New Mexico and California; Maine and Vermont. New Mexico's diversity index is 60, which means there is a 60-percent chance that any two randomly selected New Mexicans are different either racially or ethnically. California's diversity index is 59. Maine's and Vermont's diversity indexes are 4. Source: USA Today, April 11, 1991. Diversity Index developed from 1990 Census statistics by Phillip Meyer.

5. How many people indicated they were "multi-racial" in the 2010 Census? **Answer:** Over 9 million Americans took advantage of the first opportunity to check off more than one race on their 2000 census forms. More than 40 percent of those who did so were younger than 18, proof that the American populace will be even more diverse in decades to come. Some businesses see that as a signal to start broadening their messages now. Source: https://www.census.gov/prod/cen2010/briefs/c 2010br-13.pdf

6. Women make up _____ percent of all shoppers in the US; they spend ____ cents of every dollar. (fill in the blanks) **Answer:** Women make up 73 percent of all shoppers in the US; they spend 80 cents of every dollar according to www.Diversitycentral.com

7. By the year 2050, what percent of the total
United States population will Asians,
Hispanics, Blacks, and other nonwhite groups
represent? **Answer:** 47 percent. Source: "A
Spicer Stew for the Melting Pot", Business
Week, December 21, 1992.

8. What demographic group represents the fastest
growing customer base in the United States?
Answer: Hispanics. Trudy Suchan, a
cartographer in the Census bureau's
population division who helped publish a new
atlas, said she thought the atlas showed "a
surprising reach of the Hispanic population.
We tend to think of the Hispanic population as
existing only in the West and the Southwest.
.But this picture shows a greater reach."
Source: www.Diversityinc.com August 10,
2001.

9. What are the top six frequently cited barriers to advancement listed by women in the workplace? **Answer:**
   - Lack of mentoring opportunities
   - Commitment to personal and family responsibilities
   - Exclusion from informal networks of communication
   - Lack of women role models
   - Failure of senior leadership to assume accountability for women's advancement
   - Stereotyping and preconceptions of women's roles and abilities

   Source: Catalyst Newsletter, July, 2001, www.catalystwomen.org

10. One out of _____ black households makes more than $50,000 per year? Answer: 1 out of 8 (13 percent)

References

Chang, Richard, Capitalizing on Workplace Diversity, Richard Chang Associates Publications, Irvine, California, 1996.

Dupont, Kay, Handling Diversity in the Workplace, American Media Publishing, West Des Moines, Iowa, 1997.

Hubbard, Edward E., How to Calculate Diversity Return on Investment, Global Insights Publishers, Petaluma, California, 1999.

Hubbard, Edward E., "Techniques for Managing a Diverse Workforce", Global Insights Publishing, Petaluma, CA, 2002.

Humphreys, Jeffrey M., Georgia Business and Economic Conditions Journal, "The Multi-cultural Economy 2002: Minority Buying Power in the New Century, Volume 62, Number 2, Second Quarter 2002.

Loden, Marilyn, Implementing Diversity, Irwin, Chicago, Illinois, 1996.

Diversity Activities and Training Designs, Julie O'Mara, Pfeiffer & Company, San Diego, California, 1994.

Orey, Maureen C., Successful Staffing in a Diverse Workplace, A Practical Guide to Building an Effective and Diverse Staff, Richard Change Associates, Inc., Irvine, California, 1996.

Rasmussen, Tina, The ASTD Trainer's Sourcebook: Diversity, McGraw-Hill, New York, 1996.

Wright, Ferris, Hiller & Kroll, "Competitiveness through Management of Diversity: Effects on Stock Price Valuation", Academy of Management Journal, 1995, p.272-287

Websites:

www.Diversityinc.com

www.DiversityCentral.com

http://www.bls.gov/opub/mlr/2012/01/art3full.pdf

Chapter Three: The Differences Between EEO, Affirmative Action, and Managing Diversity

Differences Between EEO, Affirmative Action and Managing Diversity

Knowing the differences between EEO, Affirmative Action (AA) and Managing Diversity (MD) is often cited as a major step forward in understanding what diversity really is. For many people, theses three concepts are synonymous, but there are a wide variety of examples to illustrate how they are very different. Some employees see it as nothing new, simply a repackaging of Affirmative Action in a

different wrapper. One of the reasons for the confusion
in the terms is the way the terms are discussed in the
media. Dr. Taylor Cox and Ruby Beale, for example,
cites a Business Week article that clearly illustrates the
media's influence and genesis for some of the
confusion: "Call it affirmative action. Or minority
outreach. Or perhaps you prefer 'managing diversity',
the newest, politically well-scrubbed name for policies
aimed at bringing minorities into the mainstream
through preferential hiring and promotion." ("Race in
the Workplace," Business Week, July 8, 1991).

The language featured in this article takes the term
"managing diversity", which is a more comprehensive
term in that it includes all types of groups and
organizational activities, and reduces it to only one
dimension of difference (race) and only one
organizational activity (affirmative action). This choice
of language was made despite the wide range of
literature that is available that would have revealed a

much broader definition of the term used by experts in the field.

The Business Week article further reduces Affirmative Action, which is defined in the executive order that created it as "systematic steps to ensure that past discrimination is remedied and that further discrimination does not occur" (Werther & Davis, 1993, p.105), to two actions: preferential hiring and promotion of minorities. To make matters worst, if you explore the article further, it suggests that racial minorities really comes down to one group, Blacks. Finally, the message that managing diversity is merely a new name for Affirmative Action is further reinforced in the article with the following statement: "To get past the emotional charge carried by Affirmative Action, some employers have embraced a new catch-phrase: managing diversity" (p.58).

This type of confusion sets up a never-ending spiral of misunderstandings and barriers to effectively managing diversity. If diversity is defined as a new version of Affirmative Action, then all of the conceptual and motivational challenges that have plagued Affirmative Action will be attached to the process of "managing diversity." They help fuel personal self-interest and a belief in maintaining the status quo theory that everyone has the opportunity to succeed. That personal, not situational, attribute determines a person's economic success or failure. In addition, the notion of self-interest refers to the fact that people will tend to resist actions or policies that they perceive will reduce their personal circumstances and support those that maintain or enhance them. When people believe that the organization's environment and systems are fair on their own, there is no wonder they believe the incorrect notion that managing diversity is the same as Affirmative Action. This failed understanding of the differences between these terms creates a whole host of problems and barriers to change in organizations.

When organizations clearly understand the differences, they move beyond Affirmative Action based profile improvement efforts that are focused solely on race and gender to a focus on the organizational environment and the degree to which the diversity of all groups is fully utilized and organizational activities and systems are adjusted to build a more inclusive process directed towards performance. The goal is no longer merely satisfying legal requirements; instead, it now expands to correctly include correcting environmental issues, improving productivity and enhancing employee morale.

By focusing on the quality of the work environment and full utilization of diverse workforce talents to improve organizational performance, "managing diversity" takes a giant step beyond Affirmative Action. Its messages of respect, inclusion, and performance can help to defuse the residue of confusion, resentment and backlash that occurs in many organizations. These concerns are made worst by our sluggish economy, massive corporate downsizing, immigration concerns over the events of the September 11th terrorist attacks (where stereotypes of specific groups of people and their beliefs were challenged), the politics of division, and in some cases, poorly executed Affirmative Action programs. Managing the effects of these events and beliefs on organizational health and performance become critical.

Profile improvement will always be important and a requirement to build an effective organizational environment. As a step in a larger process of managing diversity, it can now be seen as a means to develop the path towards opportunities such as innovation, opening new multicultural markets, effective teamwork, and the like. As a new management paradigm, managing diversity holds the organization accountable for creating a culture in which diversity thrives and is utilized to meet bottom-line performance objectives. While is it is easy to see how the goals of Equal Employment Opportunity, Affirmative Action, and diversity overlap, it is important to recognize how they are different. The following chart describes some of the key differences:

EEO/Affirmative Action	Managing Diversity
Quantitative: Focuses on demographic profile changes	**Quantitative and Qualitative:** Focuses on environmental readiness and performance improvement
Government Mandated: Imposed and often un-welcomed	**Voluntary:** Internally driven and welcomed when properly explained and understood
Remedial: Focused on changing historic patterns of discrimination	**Strategic:** Focused on increasing innovation and creating a competitive advantage

EEO/Affirmative Action	Managing Diversity
Reactive: Problem response	**Proactive:** Opportunity-driven
Beneficiaries: Protected groups	**Beneficiaries:** Everyone
Initial Step	**Follow-up Step**
Culture Change: Not required	**Culture Change:** Required
Implementation: Compliance focused	**Implementation:** Competency, performance, and accountability focused

In many respects, managing diversity is an outgrowth of the early EEO and AA efforts to end discrimination and thus ending exclusionary behavior in organizations. It is a follow-up step that many organizations initiate after some internal profile changes have already occurred. Instead of ignoring cultural differences, managing diversity efforts encourages all members of the organization to increase their knowledge about diverse cultures to assist the organization in meeting its objectives. In addition to managing diversity, valuing diversity initiatives focus on bridging gaps in respect and the understanding that exists among different cultural groups in an effort to create an inclusive workplace environment.

While the objectives of EEO, Affirmative Action, and managing diversity are complementary, they can wind up on a collision course if the purpose of each is not made clear within the organization.

Developing a comprehensive implementation plan to institutionalize diversity requires that managers as change agents must question their own assumptions and understandings about workplace diversity and what it will take to get there. It requires commitment and accountability to the changing realities of a global marketplace, a willingness to address them, and an

ability to integrate the organization's vision of future
performance through the use of all diverse assets of the
organization.

Self-Assessment

This self-assessment involves the exploration of
your own values, perceptions and expectations about
diversity. Examine how they relate to your own
behavior when you encounter people you manage who
are different from yourself. Think back on your
experiences over the last week and all of the individuals
you encountered who were different. Or, in the week to
come, complete this assessment based upon your
experience. Write your responses to the following four
questions:

1. What was your first response or impression of
   this person when you first met them?

   _____

   _____

   _____

2. Examine the specific assumptions you made
   about the other person.

   _____

   _____

3. Check the reality behind your assumptions
   (were they stereotypes, prejudice, etc.).

   _____

   _____

4. Identify what you plan to do differently about how you manage these responses.

_____

_____

5. Find commonalities and appreciate the differences between you.

_____

_____

6. Develop ways to build trust.

_____

_____

References

Cox Jr., Taylor, and Beale, Ruby L., Developing
Competency to Manage Diversity, Berrett-Koehler
Publishers, San Francisco, California, 1997.

Dupont, Kay, Handling Diversity in the
Workplace, American Media Publishing, West Des
Moines, Iowa, 1997.

Loden, Marilyn, Implementing Diversity, Irwin,
Chicago, Illinois, 1996.

Werther, W.B., & Davis, K., Human Resources
and Personnel Management, McGraw-Hill, New York,
1993.

Chapter Four: Barriers to Diversity and Inclusion

People are diverse in many ways. We have a number of differences that offer a wide range of opportunities and possibilities to make organizations successful and our world a better place. When we accept our differences and learn to work with them, we enrich our lives and improve the creativity and productivity of the organization. However, too often, organizations find they work against the effective use of differences and allow them to hinder instead of help.

Why do we have so many problems dealing with diversity? Diversity itself isn't a problem—our differences have always been there; they are what makes us unique. The problems lie in our attitudes towards diversity. People who have negative attitudes towards other people's difference often engage in negative behaviors including:

- Prejudice
- Stereotyping and Discrimination
- Ethnocentrism

To keep these negative behaviors from becoming barriers to organizational diversity, we must learn to recognize and avoid them in all types of situations such as working with employees, business relationships, customer relationships, hiring, firing, and the like. Prejudice, stereotyping and discrimination hurt people and ultimately destroy an organization's effectiveness and bottom-line. Let's explore these barriers in more detail…

Prejudice

Prejudice is a preconceived feeling or bias. Each of us has biases of one kind or another. Some people wouldn't be caught dead driving a certain make of car or wearing a certain brand of clothes. Other people may swear by that car or brand. We all have likes and dislikes. As long as our biases are about unimportant things, like our brand of toothpaste, they are relatively harmless. However, when we hold prejudices against other people, we create all kinds of problems.

Prejudice against people comes from a belief in the superiority of one's own race, culture, class, or other group. Often, prejudice takes this ethnocentric form. Although America was founded on the principle of "liberty and justice for all" and most people want to believe in equal rights, current studies show that 10 to 20 percent of Americans still express bigotry. However, there is a trend toward not openly expressing prejudice, but subliminally still viewing nontraditional employees as less competent. (Dovido, The Subtlety of Racism, 1993)

Other studies highlight the impact of prejudice even further and show that even people who want to

avoid bias are *conditioned* for a biased response. In one
experiment, executives were given resumes and photos
of job applicants and asked to describe jobs they might
offer the people. All the resumes were identical, but the
pictures were different: a white man, a black man, a
Hispanic man, a black woman, and a Hispanic woman.
White executives typically assigned administrative
tasks to the women of color and line tasks to the men of
color. Further, in an illustration of how broad reaching
prejudices can be and how it can create internalized
oppression, when women of color were given the same
assignment as the White executives, with the same
photos and resumes, they made the same job
assignments.

Another study revealed that biased behavior is
largely unconscious. People who display negative non-
verbal reactions to others are usually unaware they are
doing so. (Bass, "Bias Below the Surface," The
Washington Post, 1990) One of the most devastating
aspects of prejudice is that people deny they have

biases. Denying it only perpetuates the problem. It can also be related to a sense of not wanting to admit to a "loss of control" similar to incidents when people get lost and need directions. Often, they do not want to admit that they are lost and certainly don't want to admit it to a stranger!

At other times, prejudice can come in the form of "backlash" when people perceive diversity as nothing but an attempt to fill quotas and take jobs away from others. When this mindset exists, resentment, poor teamwork, and sabotage can result that affects productivity. Some prejudice is a matter of blind conformity to prevailing cultural beliefs and customs. However, in most cases prejudice seems to fulfill a specific irrational function for people such as making them feel superior to others, or using others as scapegoats for the prejudiced persons' own resentment or guilt. Prejudice usually is tied to a person's deepest fears, although the connection is normally subconscious and therefore hidden from awareness. Researchers have uncovered some interesting facts about prejudice:

- Prejudice is found in all types of people in every ethnic group
- Prejudice occurs in the mind but can be acted out in ways that exclude others
- Prejudiced acts can be performed by non-prejudiced as well as prejudiced people
- The best way to decide if an action is prejudiced is to notice how it affects another person. You can't prove someone is prejudiced, but you may prove that his or her actions excluded and placed another person at a disadvantage.

We talk about prejudice in terms of workplace prejudice, sexism, racism, ethnic prejudice, and other "isms". Workplace prejudice is active in organizational workplaces today. According to the National Opinion Research Center, some people still believe the stereotypes that women and ethnic minorities are less intelligent, less hard-working, less likely to be self supporting, more violence-prone, and less patriotic than

they are. Organizations such as the U.S. Glass Ceiling
Commission and Catalyst have stated in their research
reports that prejudice is the biggest barrier to
advancement that diverse employees face.

Sexism

Sexism is prejudice based on gender and is said by
some to be the root of all prejudice and discrimination.
As children we literally begin learning this form of
inequality in the cradle. It doesn't involve a majority
and minority, since men and women are relatively equal
in number. However, women in all countries are a
minority in economic and political arenas and have
fewer rights and privileges than men.

Racism

Racism is typically a problem in societies such as
the United States, where there is a predominant

majority group and one or more cultural minorities. People often use the term racism in discussions of prejudice. The term "race" has little meaning in anthropology. Because of intermarriages, you can have some experts say there are 3 races and others say there are 300. This fact notwithstanding, a major explanation for discrimination in society takes place in the name of race.

Ethnic Prejudice

People who try to distinguish between race and ethnicity typically say that racial traits are inborn, inherited, and given by nature, while ethnic traits are learned, cultural, and acquired through nurture. Since most of the characteristics vary from culture to culture are learned and are not permanently fixed in our genes, they can theoretically be changed. "Ethnicity" is much more flexible and changeable than "race."

An ethnic subculture is a segment of a larger culture or society. Members of the subculture participate in shared activities in which the common origin and culture are significant ingredients. A subculture is unique because of its particular beliefs, customs and values, its heroes and heroines, its myths and stories, and its social networks. Ethnic discrimination against minorities occurs when "minority" status carries with it the exclusion from full participation in the society and the largest subculture holds an undue share of power, influence and wealth.

Other Isms

Other isms include ageism, classism, or class snobbery, and homophobia, or antigay prejudice. Besides ethnic minorities and women, groups that experience discrimination in the workplace include persons with disabilities, gay people, older employees, and obese people. To a lesser extent, people from lower socioeconomic groups may be targets of prejudice, as symbolized by such derogatory terms as "trailer trash", and "poor White trash". Prejudice knows no boundaries, however, and some people believe that all post office employees are deadbeat bureaucrats, all administrators are corrupt political sharks, and so on.

Self-Assessment: Being Tolerated Versus Being Appreciated

Purpose: To experience the difference between tolerance and appreciation.

Step One: Being Tolerated

- Think of a time when you felt tolerated. Write a few words about it.

- How did it feel to be merely tolerated? Write a
  few words about your feelings

- How did feeling tolerated affect your
  relationship with the tolerant person (s)?

- If it was a job situation, how motivated and
  effective were you after you realized you were
  being tolerated?

Step Two: Being Appreciated

- Think of a time when you felt appreciated.
  Write a few words about it.

_____

_____

- How did it feel to be truly appreciated? Did
  you feel respected? Write a few words about
  your feelings

_____

_____

- How did feeling appreciated affect your
  relationship with the appreciative person(s)?

_____

_____

- If it was a job situation, how motivated and
  effective were you after you realized you were
  truly appreciated?

_____

_____

- Based upon this exercise, what are the lessons
  learned and/or what would you change in your
  own behavior from this point forward?

_____

_____

Stereotyping and Discrimination

As we discussed earlier, stereotypes are defined as
fixed, inflexible notions about a group. Stereotyping
occurs when we apply our biases to all members of a
group. If you were raised to think all members of a

particular ethnic group are lazy, you may still hold this stereotype, no matter what your day-to-day experience tells you. If you believe strongly in this stereotype, you may also spread it to others. A more technical look at stereotyping finds that it is a process that allows us to manage complex realities using categories to store information, to quickly identify things, to handle multi-sensory experiences and make sense out of things. We often attach strong emotions to these stereotypes, even when they're false, and often use stereotypes to justify our dislike of someone.

We stereotype when we apply an experience with one member of a group to the entire group. If you met one member of a particular culture who was rude in the way they treated you, it might be hard for you to recognize that not everyone from that particular group behaves in a rude way. But just because one member of a race, gender, age group, or culture acts a certain way doesn't mean every other person of that group will act the same way. Your perceptions could be based on a lack of knowledge because you haven't taken the time to understand the other person's culture. Many stereotypical generalizations are based upon misconception and errors in judgment.

Sometimes people generalize too much or stereotype simply because they do not have the facts, have limited personal experience, or are working with distorted information. Stereotypes often lead to assumptions that are insupportable and offensive. They cloud the fact that all attributes may be found in all groups and individuals. Stereotypes show up in phrases like "men won't ask for directions" or "you know 'those people' can't handle responsibility at this level". The stereotypes we attach to people hurt us as much as they hurt everybody else, because we can't get to know other people for who they really are. However, we can change when we discover how this stereotyping behavior develops.

When we stereotype, we form large classes and clusters of information for guiding our daily adjustments to life. We must deal with a lot of complexity in our lives and often need a process for sorting things out. We may not feel that we have time to get to know everyone and every situation, so we "generalize, delete, and distort" information to align it with information in broad categories for sanity sake. Unfortunately, we may associate this information with old categories just to make sense of the world. By doing so however, it can prevent us from being completely open-minded.

These categories become our short cuts. We tend to place as much as we can in these classes and clusters to categorize events to take action. We are "inference focus beings" that like to solve problems. When left with little or no data, we will generalize, delete and distort to come up with an answer to solve a problem or make sense of a person or situation. Because we like to problem solve as easy as possible, we try to fit things together rapidly into a satisfactory category and use this category as a means of judging what it is or means.

A stereotype enables us to readily identify related things. Stereotypes have a close and immediate tie with what we see, how we judge, and what actions we take. In fact, their whole purpose is to help us make responses and adjustments to life in a speedy, smooth, and consistent manner. For each mental category we create, we have a thinking and feeling tone or flavor. Everything in that category takes on that flavor. For example, we not only know what the term "Southern Belle" means, we also have a feeling tone that is favorable or unfavorable that immediately comes to mind along with this concept. When we meet someone that we decide is a "Southern Belle", that feeling tone determines whether we like her more or less than we would if we got to know her on her own merits. Does "labeling" her as a "Southern Belle" cause you to instantly predict that this experience will be pleasurable or a pain?

Rationality and Justifying Our Fear

Stereotypes may be more or less rational. A
rational stereotype starts to grow from a kernel or truth
and enlarges and solidifies with each new relevant
experience. A rational stereotype gives us information
that we think can help us predict how someone will
behave or what might happen in a situation. An
irrational stereotype is one we've formed without
adequate evidence. When you add emotions to this
mixture, your get an overwhelmingly powerful sense of
conviction about something that may or may not be
based in truth. An irrational idea that is engulfed by an
overpowering emotion is more likely to conform to the
emotion than to objective evidence. Therefore, once we
develop an irrational stereotype that we feel strongly
about, its difficult for us to change that stereotype based
upon facts alone. We must deal with the emotion and its
ties to our deepest fears.

Sometimes we form stereotypes that are linked to an emotion related to fear such as hostility, suspicion, dislike, or disgust and set up the framework for prejudice towards an entire group of people based upon our experience with one person or a few people. When people become prejudiced toward a group, they need to justify their dislike, and any justification that fits the immediate conversational situation will do. We constantly make others prove us wrong in our negative assumptions, rather than assuming the best. In addition, when people don't fit the stereotype, we think they're the exception rather than questioning our stereotype of them or the group they belong to.

Stereotyping is a double edge sword. On one hand, it allows you to handle a world full of multi-sensory data such that you do not become overwhelmed, however left on its own without a conscious understanding of how it affects the way we categorize, it can be fatally problematic. When our categorizations become too fixed, our labels too permanent, and our

perceptions too rigid, it often leads to prejudice and
discrimination against people.

Discrimination

Discrimination does not mean failing to hire
enough women, minorities, or gays; it doesn't even
mean refusing to associate with people from other
cultures. Discrimination is treating people different,
unequally, and usually negatively because they are
members of a particular group. We develop prejudices,
turn them into stereotypes, and allow them to grow into
discrimination. Unfortunately, prejudice, stereotyping,
and discrimination are still facts of organizational life
and our society with all of the associated negative
consequences. We see these diversity barriers in the
form of racist or sexist jokes, rude remarks, or the
refusal to hire or promote. If you encountered a person
being discriminated against today, how would you
handle it? Keep in mind doing nothing is taking a
position.

What's Your Experience?

Have you ever been discriminated against? Have you ever witnessed someone being discriminated against? If so, what did you do?

My Experience:

Situations I Witnessed. What I Did.

If others you know are discriminatory and you accept that part of them without protest, you are actually allowing discrimination to continue. You can discriminate merely being a part of an organization that itself unintentionally discriminates through its traditional business practices. This can come about due to a power-privilege imbalance that automatically favors a dominant majority and is unfavorable to minorities. Unfavorable, that is, until some actions are taken to offset and correct this imbalance. The press is filled with cases that highlight organizational inability to deal effectively with diversity and the financial and other costs incurred.

- Racial bias claims alone cost the American Economy about $215 billion a year. That's almost 4 percent of the gross domestic product (GDP)

- More than one-third of the Fortune 500 companies have been sued for sexual harassment, many of them more than once. A

Working Women magazine survey of Fortune
500 businesses as far back as 1988 determined
that the direct costs of sexual harassment
averaged $6.7 million in lost productivity,
absenteeism, and turnover annually per
company. One expert estimates that when
overall gender bias is figured in, organizations
lose over $15 million per year.

- Age discrimination cases are up since the Age
  Discrimination Act went into effect in 1987,
  with a median of $219,000 awarded in
  successful suits.

- Disability claims have also been rising since
  the Americans with Disabilities Act went into
  effect in 1992. It is having a major effect on
  the way organizations do business by adjusting
  access to include all available talent.

- Court costs, attorney fees, settlements, stress
  related illnesses due to hostile work
  environment, poor productivity, poor quality,
  impacts on short term and long-term disability

insurance expenses, impact on customer
service level maintenance and ability to
compete must also be included in the cost side
of the ledger.

A power imbalance is a key aspect of discrimination. Power is a force that is absolutely essential to perpetuate discrimination. For example, an African American clerk may dislike a White executive and never try to get to know him as a person. Her actions are not called "discrimination" because she does not have the power to take actions that exclude him in ways that disadvantage his career. On the other hand, the executive does have the power to discriminate against her, and that type of power differential is not unusual. White men still hold nearly all of the top-level economic and political power in the United States. They hold 92 percent of the top-level positions in mid to large-sized businesses and about 80 percent of the seats in Congress, even though they comprise only approximately 35 percent of the population and 39 percent of the workforce, according to the U.S. Census Bureau and the U.S. Glass Ceiling Commission. Civil rights measures are based upon the fact that a power imbalance exists and represents an attempt to break the cycle of centuries of discrimination.

Discrimination against diverse workforce employees not only affects their career progress, it also affects their trust, motivation, and productivity in addition to their relationships with the rest of the workforce. It affects them in every phase and aspect of their work experience. These include areas such as:

- **Recruitment Practices** – Examples include unwillingness to hire people who are different, selective advertising of high-level positions in media rarely used by minorities, etc.

- **Screening Practices** - Examples include using preferences as if they are real requirements to be effective in the job, stereotyping intelligence attributes to different groups, prejudices against education received at specific minority-focused colleges or universities, vague or arbitrary assessments made by others who may be prejudiced in their view then using that assessment to determine who will be interviewed.

- **Terms and Conditions of Employment** – Examples include the fact that women and minorities typically earn about 70 percent of white male salaries for the same job with equivalent experience, may receive fewer benefits, fewer opportunities to be in succession plans and development or mentoring experiences.

- **Tracking and Job Segregation** – Examples include "women jobs", "men jobs", and "minority jobs" even though in today's "politically correct" environment they would never be called that.

- **Performance Evaluation** – Examples include the way job performance of women and minorities is viewed versus others. Successful performance by women and African American men on tasks traditionally done by white males tends to be attributed to luck, while white men's performance is more likely attributed to their abilities according to the research of J. H Greenhaus and S. Parasuraman. Minorities and women are often held to a more limited range of acceptable behavior than others. Assertive behavior for example may be viewed negatively if exhibited by a woman or a person of color.

- **Promotion Practices** – Examples include unwritten, informal rules or expectations that are rarely shared and administered equally for women and minorities, prejudging a women's career potential based upon her family status.

- **Glass Ceilings, Sticky Floors, and Compressed Walls** – Examples include

research that shows white men at the top of
organizations prefer colleagues of their same
gender and race. Clear statistical evidence that
shows multi-year patterns that of poor
development, succession planning, promotion
and retention of high-level minority and
women executives.

- **Diverse Standards** – Such as "not aggressive
  enough", "lacks initiative", "too passive" or
  "too emotional" when the real reason is
  misreading a person's cultural traits.

- **Layoff, Discharge, and Seniority Practices**
  – Examples include protecting workers who
  have been there the longest knowing that
  minorities and women are often the last hire
  and the first fired or laid off, or cannot get
  into the trades and other programs to meet
  seniority requirements. In some cases,
  minorities have been barred from certain
  occupations.

- **Career Alternatives** – Discrimination can
  make it even more difficult for diverse
  employees to choose alternatives to corporate
  careers that hit a glass ceiling. Many women
  and minorities, in general, may have fewer
  assets and more difficulty in getting business
  loans than do white men, however this is
  changing.

Self-Assessment: How Privileged Are You

Please respond to the following questions:

1. What are some privileges you enjoy in life?
   List a few.

_____

_____

2. How do privileges affect your life? Do they
   affect you personal power? Your ability to
   achieve your goals? Your success?

_____

_____

3. Which of these (or other) privileges are
   unavailable to some people because of the
   group they belong to? Beside each unavailable
   privilege, write the name of the group(s) who
   don't enjoy these privileges.

Privileges Unavailable Others	Group(s) that don't Enjoy this Privilege

4. What are some privileges that are unavailable
to you that people from certain groups enjoy?
List each privilege and beside it, the group or
groups that have access to it.

Privileges Unavailable Me	Group(s) that have Access to this Privilege

<table>
<tr><td></td><td></td></tr>
</table>

5. How does this lack of privilege affect your
life? Your personal power? Your ability to
achieve your goals? Your success?

Ethnocentrism

Another barrier to diversity that shows up in the
workplace is "ethnocentric" behavior. Ethnocentrism is
the belief that a person's own group is inherently
superior to all others. People who exhibit ethnocentric
behavior have a "my way or the highway" attitude that
negates anyone else's opinion as worth considering.

Ethnocentrism, like prejudice, stereotypes, and discrimination places barriers in the way of performance for those considered in the "out group". In order to be effective, ethnocentrism must be rooted out of the organization. It is counter-productive to high performance and dampens efforts of creativity and innovation.

Non-Verbal Communication

Our "non-verbal communication" or "body language" can be another obstacle to a diverse, high-performance work environment. Our actions do in fact speak louder than words. When people know us as individuals, our unspoken words my be understood and therefore they may not respond to a gesture, a type of eye contact, or "odd" movement as threatening or negative. However, someone from another race, gender, culture, age or economic background might easily misinterpret them. Although our world is becoming smaller, we never all share the same language, culture or mannerisms. No gestures are universal. Worse yet, sometimes our tongues say one thing, our gestures say another thing and our symbols (clothing, jewelry, hairstyles, facial hair, body markings) say still another thing. Mixed signals can be very misleading to other people, especially people who come from an area where the words, gestures, or symbols mean something entirely different.

Gestures

Have you ever folded your arms, flashed a victory sign, extended your left hand to someone as a handshake, made direct eye contact with someone while talking, etc? If you have, you have offended someone in a particular culture. For example, the victory sign shown with the palm inward is an insult with vulgar overtones to Australians. It's easy to offend someone without even knowing it.

The gestures that mean, "okay" to people born and raised in the United States have various meanings in other countries. To coworker from Japan, for example, it means "money". To business associates who grew up in France, Belgium, and Tunisia, it signals "worthless", or "zero". To those from Turkey, Greece, and Malta, it refers to Homosexuality. To people who grew up in the rest of Europe and Mexico, this gesture represents an obscene or lewd comment. The crooked finger that native-born Americans use to say "Come here" is also considered obscene in many cultures. It's often the way people call prostitutes, animals, or "inferior" people! So it is easy to see that you could insult someone from another culture without even knowing it or why it might have been offensive.

Movement

Something as simple as how we sit and the position of our body can communicate a negative message. For example, people with a European heritage are sometimes offended by the way American men cross their legs while sitting. From their perspective, it is considered crude. Americans on the other hand may consider some European men effeminate due to the way they cross their legs and the lack of firmness in their handshake.

Even when you talk with Americans, there are different messages communicated by the way people in America sit, stand, shake hands or cross their legs. There is plenty of room for things to be misunderstood. A women with her arms crossed around her chest may not signal that she is closed to anything you have to say, she could be cold or it could simply the way she likes to stand. A person with a weak handshake may have arthritis or some other malady that affects the strength of their handshake.

Personal Space

People often have their own comfort zones with distances from themselves. Have you ever watched what happens to a person's level of comfort when they are in a crowded elevator? Ever notice how close or far away people stand to senior executives if they are first-level employees? Have you ever approached someone and had him/her back away from you? It might be that people from this person's culture don't like having people close to them whereas you may have been raised to stand close to someone. Here are some comfort zone distances that have been found to be true among certain cultures:

- Americans – 8 inches to 3 feet
- Mexican Americans – closeness up to 18 inches
- Japanese Americans – 3 to 6 feet

Often, people may not consciously set these social distances, however, they just know that when others come close, they feel uncomfortable. Nonetheless, personal space is always based upon the needs of the other person. You should pay close attention to how another person responds in words, tone and inflection, and body language. If that person winces, backs up, looks confused or worried, etc., be honest, ask if there is anything you are doing that is making them uncomfortable.

Eye Contact and Touching

Eye contact follows the same rules as personal space. In American culture, it is not unusual for people to maintain eye contact for extended periods of time. It reflects a sense of power and confidence. In many cultures, however (especially Asian, Mexican, Latin American, Native American and Caribbean), less eye contact is more respectful. Many African Americans were also raised this way. When some managers do not get a direct gaze from their employees, customers, or co-workers, they view these individuals as less confident and perhaps timid. This may even get interpreted as if the person has done wrong or something they are guilty or ashamed of. Of course, jumping to these conclusions based upon these

observations leads to all kinds of misunderstandings
and poor performance.

Touching is another sensitive area. Some managers
feel that due to their position of authority, they can
touch employees without causing people to be
offended, however, they may become offended if a
member of their support team touched them or stood
too closely. The rules of equality say that we should not
use a behavior without being willing to receive it as
well and most importantly; it must not violate the rules
of sexual harassment. Shaking hands is always a polite
way to greet people in America, and occasionally, a pat
on the back. In some other countries, touching is
forbidden or discouraged. In many Asian countries,
body contact is considered disrespectful; instead, a nod
or bow is more appropriate.

Sense of Time

Many people and cultures have different
sensitivities to time. The notion of "being on time" has

a number of different meanings. In some countries arriving at an appointment at exactly the agreed upon time is considered late, especially if the expectation is that you should always arrive at least 10 minutes early. In other countries, arriving one-half hour after the appointed time is fine since time is viewed as relative. Many Mexican Americans consider themselves punctual up to 30 minutes past the scheduled time.

Punctuality is highly valued by business-oriented Americans. They rush to and from everything and place a high priority on meeting deadlines. To people from other cultures and upbringings, however, time may have less significance. Native Americans, for instance, believe that since you can't be in two places at once, you should be wherever you are needed when you are needed rather than be governed by the clock. This doesn't mean that they disregard time or schedules, its just that they value the concept of time differently.

You might ask, how could anything get done if everyone has different ideas about time? In a business meeting, everyone should be slightly flexible but should not be expected to wait very long. Accepted protocol says that 15 minutes is long enough to wait for an appointment in the U.S. If you have somewhere else to go or do, leave a note explaining that you waited as long as you could and will reschedule as soon as possible.

It is important to understand each person's sensitivities and its impact on organizational performance. When you are able to understand and respect things from their cultural perspective, it will help you avoid some of the major interpersonal barriers to diversity. The costs of these interpersonal missteps go far beyond any financial expenses.

Accepting Differences

As long as we are all different, there will not be one standard of behavior that will be identical. What is appropriate for one person or one culture will not be appropriate for another. Our values, beliefs, and customs will highlight significant differences in communication that signal whether someone is perceived as being respected or not. The concept of "independence", for example, is emphasized in American culture, so people grow up with the value and belief that mobility is OK. Friendships may be fleeting and possibly short term (the norm). However, more traditional cultures emphasize family and long-term relationships (the norm). People who grew up in European, Asian and other cultures don't move around quickly or easily. They are often born and die in the same city, town, or village. They tend to take time to get to know people for the long-term. So for example if you are friendly at work, some people from more

traditional cultures may not understand why you don't
invite them to socialize outside of work.

When the workplace is diverse with people who
have different standards, values, and beliefs for how
relationships are formed, it can cause challenges,
misunderstandings and an unfriendly work
environment. One person might appear pushy while
another may seem formal and distant. How people
socialize, what constitutes teamwork, what serves as a
reward or not will be dictated by our differences. To be
effective in eliminating barriers and handling the
challenges of managing in an increasingly multicultural
and global society, you will need to be highly
competent in the use of a wide range of
communications skills.

Self-Assessment: Identifying Organizational Barriers to Diversity

Instructions: Rank-order the following list of
barriers to diversity that you perceive in your
organization. The most significant barrier ranks as "1"
in the list and the least important a "10".

Rank	Barrier
	Fear of hiring less qualified, under skilled, uneducated employees
	Strong belief that the current system is already fair to everyone
	Culture where stereotypes and prejudice towards different groups (such as race, gender, ethnicity, sexual preferences, age, etc.) is significant
	Diversity is not seen as a strategic priority for the organization

	Reluctance to dismantle existing systems to integrate diversity
	Few diversity champions willing to take a leadership role
	Perception that there has been a lot of progress in diversity already
	Confusion over the difference between Managing Diversity, EEO and Affirmative Action
	Cost of implementing a diversity effort
	Concerns of being sued if attention is brought to this issue

Adapted from Gardenswartz and Rowe, The Diversity Survival Guide

Interpreting Your Answers

As you review your answers to your prioritized list ask yourself the following questions:

- Are there any barriers you would like to add that were not found on the list?
- What is the impact of the organization of not dealing with each of these barriers?
- Based on answers to the last question, which three barriers are the most significant or costly?
- What do you see happening to morale and productivity if you do nothing?
- What needs to happen in order to tear down some of these barriers?
- Where is a good place to begin?

References

Carr-Ruffino, Norma, Diversity Success Strategies, Butterworth Heinemann Publishers, Boston, MA, 1999.

Dupont, Kay, Handling Diversity in the Workplace, American Media Publishing, West Des Moines, Iowa, 1997.

Gardenswartz, Lee, Rowe, Anita "The Managing Diversity Survival Guide", McGraw-Hill, Boston, MA, 1994

Greenhaus, J.H. and S. Parasuraman, "Job Performance Attributions and Career Advancement Prospects", Organizational Behavior and Decision Processes, Academic Press, Orlando, Florida, 1991.

Hubbard, Edward E., "Techniques for Managing a Diverse Workforce", Global Insights Publishing, Petaluma, CA, 2002.

Kennedy, Debbe, "Assessment: Defining Current Realities", Berrett-Koehler Communications, San Francisco, CA, 2000.

Kennedy, Debbe, "Achievement: Measuring Progress; Celebrating Success", Berrett-Koehler Communications, San Francisco, CA, 2000.

Morrison, Ann, The New Leaders, Guidelines on Leadership Diversity in America, Jossey-Bass, San Francisco, California, 1992.

National Opinion Research Center, Ethnic Images, GSS Topical Report No.19, Chicago: University of Chicago, December, 1990.

Rasmussen, Tina, The ASTD Trainer's Sourcebook: Diversity, McGraw-Hill, New York, 1996.

Chapter Five:
Developing
Competencies for
Managing Diversity

Introduction

When it comes to managing diversity, many managers
often ask, "when I'm managing a diverse work group,
what am I suppose to do that is different than managing
any other group?" This is certainly a legitimate question
and deserves an answer. Manager often feel that any
preparation they have had to perform the primary
management tasks of "Planning", "Organizing",
"Directing", and "Controlling" should be more than
enough to handle any situation. It is certainly true that
these skills and competencies will go a long way in
assisting a manager to accomplish organizational work,

however, managing diversity requires additional
awareness, knowledge and skills to be effective.

For managers to lead diverse staffs and create inclusive,
productive work groups, they need information and
abilities on three levels: awareness, knowledge, and
skills. First they need awareness about their own
comfort with differences as well as their assumptions
about those differences.

Beyond awareness of your own subtle expectations,
there is a need for knowledge about different cultural
norms, lifestyle needs, and personal preferences of
individuals from different groups. For example, you
might ponder "Why do some employees speak their
native languages at work even when they know
English?"

Finally, managers have skill needs in the area of
management responsibilities such as giving feedback,
reviewing performance, and building productive work

teams (Gardenswartz and Rowe). They need answers to
skill-related situations and questions such as:

- **Situation:** A physician gives directions to a
  Filipino nurse. When he asks if she
  understands the procedure, she nods her head
  and says yes. Later, the physician notices her
  doing the procedure incorrectly. In
  exasperation he asks, "Why didn't you tell me
  if you didn't understand?" How can I give
  directions to someone who won't tell me when
  he/she doesn't understand?

- **Question:** How can I give a performance
  review that does not cause a decline in
  motivation because of hurt feelings?

- **Question:** How can I keep my staff from
  segregating into separate ethnic, racial or
  gender groupings?

- **Question:** What training and development
  needs do I have regarding my needs for

awareness, knowledge, and skills related to
effectively managing diversity?

- **Situation:** A manager who becomes angry
  because one of his Latino employees takes the
  day off each time his wife needs to go to a
  doctor's appointment. The manager cannot
  understand the need to do this, since he has
  been told in other situations that the
  employee's wife drives and takes care of
  shopping and other errands on her own.

Awareness

Reflections Exercise

Take a moment to picture in your mind each of the
following individuals:

- A Law Enforcement Officer

- A successful Corporate Executive
- A great Artist
- A renowned Heart Surgeon
- A master Burglar
- A Secretary
- A Welfare Recipient
- A Classics Professor
- A Migrant Farm Worker
- A Nurse
- A Drug Dealer
- A Computer Whiz

What does each of them look like in your mind's eye? What was their race or ethnicity? What was their gender? How tall or short were they? How stout or skinny were they? What was the color of their hair? Did they wear glasses? Were their clothes crisp and neat or wrinkled and ragged? How old was each individual. Did they have any apparent physical disabilities? If you heard their voice, what would they sound like? What did you feel (any physical sensations-uneasy, angry, annoyed, comfortable, trusting, etc.) just thinking about a person with this label? If you are like most people, your visual images, auditory recollections, and emotional state may be fueled by various stereotypes, some of them based upon race and gender. You are rare indeed if your nurse or secretary wasn't a woman, your classics professor a tweedy, white male- or your welfare recipient a portly Black or Hispanic woman.

The point I am making is that the instant perceptions we form of others often determine the course we will take as we interaction with them. This often before even a single word is spoken or a handshake takes place. And if that is the case, this process has all kinds of implications for affecting fair and equitable treatment for all employees, especially women and minorities. It could affect a person's ability to see clearly and compassionately during a conversational exchange and affect the outcome. It may affect how fully these individuals will be able to contribute to the bottom-line, by providing ideas, suggestions, problem-solving approaches, process changes, make a business case for new products and services for non-traditional markets (Fernandez, 1999).

In other words, due to our cultural software programming and lack of awareness, judgments that may be based upon racist or sexist stereotypes will clearly inhibit successful interactions among managers, employees, customers and others because it undercuts trust and respect. We cannot build up trust and respect on the basis of incorrect or incomplete information about the people we are trying to interact with. It is not healthy for either party and the consequences can be deadly and costly to the organization. The impact includes misunderstandings, resentment, low morale, poor productivity, lawsuits, rampant mistakes, customer dissatisfaction, and under-served markets.

When managing diversity, cultural programming often creates people who suffer from what I call the "*No-Knows*", that is, "the things they don't know they

are supposed to know." For example, if you don't know
that you are suppose to know how to recognize and
respond to someone who won't tell you he/she doesn't
understand, then how do you find out that you should
have known that? Confusing? It can be, especially if
you have been raised in an environment where the norm
was "if someone didn't understand something, it is up
to him or her to speak up and say so." The culture we
grow up in represents "behavioral software" that
programs our perceptions of what is "the normal or
natural way of doing things". It creates the lenses we
use to perceive the world and strongly influences the
choices we view for the "right way to behave" in a
particular situation.

All of us are programmed by cultural "software"
that determines our behavior and attitudes, from our
response in making eye contact with someone, whom
we choose to give a smile, how we deal with conflict,
and the choice of words we use to describe someone.
Cultural programming guides our behavior. Without

this programming we would be as useless as a computer without software. Our culturally programmed awareness teaches us how to interact with one another, how to solve life's daily problems, and, in effect, how to move through and control the world around us. No society exists without these rules, and no individual is culture-free.

Our culture is more than manners. It drives, directs and selects the subtlest aspects of our behavior, such as how long to wait between sentences, when it is okay to interrupt someone, and how to interpret the look on someone's face. Though most cultural rules are never written, they are all the more powerful because they are absorbed unconsciously as we watch others and their reactions to us.

It is easy for us to accept and understand that while we may eat cereal and juice for breakfast, someone else is having tortillas, rice, grits, ham hocks, or black coffee and cigarettes. However, when it comes to interpreting each other's behavior, cultural differences make understanding more difficult. To make matters worse, when we interpret another person's behavior through our own "cultural perceptual filters" (our software), we make mistakes. We take the nodding head to mean, "I understand", rather than "Yes, I heard you" as in the case of the Filipino nurse. We think the quick smile means the person is friendly and affable, rather than thinking he or she may be uncomfortable and perhaps embarrassed by our behavior or his or her own confusion. Or we assume that the employee who does not speak out in staff meetings is not a "go-getter", not assertive, or worse yet is stupid when in fact he or she may be showing you respect by keeping his or her ideas to himself or herself to honor your status and level.

How does this misinterpretation happen? Generally it happens through a lack of awareness, knowledge, and understanding. According to Adler and Kiggunder, when we encounter another's behavior, we need to make sense of it, so we follow a three-step process. First, we describe what we see, as in the case of a Latino employee: "This employee has refused a promotion to a management position." Second, we interpret the behavior: "He is not interested in getting ahead and missing a wonderful opportunity." Third, we make an evaluation: "He is lacking initiative, ungrateful for this opportunity, lacks confidence, or any combination of these."

Steps two and three are the ones that get us in trouble in our intercultural interactions. A critical step in bridging the gap is learning more about other cultures' programming so that we can avoid making incorrect assumptions about someone's behavior. For example, if you knew that the individual in the previous scenario was a young Mexican immigrant, you would consider that he might be avoiding the promotion because in his culture, being a part of a group is more important than advancement or because it would put him in a supervisory position over his friends and / or

an older man from his same culture. Since by his
norms, elders are respected and promotions are made
by age, he would be very uncomfortable being forced to
embarrass himself and his older compatriot by giving
the older worker orders.

Our awareness is based in large part upon the basic
cultural programming we received during our
developmental years. Therefore our software and lenses
are a product of the values and beliefs we learned from
life-learning sources such as home, church, school,
state, peer-group, etc. This creates a "bias", mental
leaning, or inclination to see things a particular way.
We become partial to lenses that reflect a certain point
of view. Over time, this point of view can harden into
"stereotypes" or fixed notions and mental patterns that
generate assumptions about what we should consider
"normal" and "different".

If these stereotypes are left unchecked, they can
develop into "prejudice." That is, they take the form of

a judgment or opinion formed before any real facts are known, usually as an unfavorable preconceived idea that is held in spite of facts to the contrary. Worse still, this prejudice can lead to "discrimination." Discrimination takes place when we make distinctions in treatment; show partiality in favor of or prejudice against someone or something. Ultimately, it can lead to "racism" and other "isms" such as sexism, classism, ageism, etc. At this level, our behavior can reflect programs (institutionalized) and practices of racial and other discrimination, segregation, persecution, and domination.

Therefore, the first stage in any learning process to develop competency for managing diversity is to first become self-aware. For example, to begin your own self-awareness journey you might ask: "What are my unconscious expectations of African Americans? Latinos and Latinas? Women?" "Am I surprised when secretaries or nurses aren't women, or when I meet doctors or executives who are?" This includes

becoming aware of your own cultural programming and
your own limitations.

Self-Assessment: Understanding Your Cultural Programming and Others

Instructions: This is an exercise to identify the
influences that may have played a role in your cultural
programming and to strengthen your self- and general-
awareness. It is broken into two parts. Part One asks
you to reflect on the influences that played a role in
your development over the years to the best of your
knowledge. When responding to the "Next 5 Years"
section, you are being asked to forecast what might be
true for you during that period.

Part Two asks you to reflect on your knowledge of
generational influences. Based upon the birth years
below, fill in as much information as you can that

address the items listed. Begin by filling in responses for the period of your birth year. Then list what you know about the other years listed. A few ideas are listed as examples.

Part One: Your Developmental Influences

Identify the influences you have experienced during the following periods:

Period	0-12 Years Old	13-20 Years Old	21-Today	Next 5 Years
Important Values and Beliefs: ** List your top 3-5 values				

Period	0-12 Years Old	13-20 Years Old	21-Today	Next 5 Years
and beliefs that guided your life during this period				
**Changes over time?				
**Events Driving the Change?				
**Diversity Management Implications?				

Period	0-12 Years Old	13-20 Years Old	21-Today	Next 5 Years
**Who Were Your heroes?				
**Religious Affiliation(s)				
**Income Status: Low, Middle, Affluent				
Neighborhood: **Same				

Period	0-12 Years Old	13-20 Years Old	21-Today	Next 5 Years
**Mixed (25% or more of other groups)				
Close Friends: **Same **Mixed (25% or more of other groups)				

Part Two: Generational Influences

List the information for your birth year first, then add what you know about others

Birth Years	1922-1943	1943-1960	1960-1980	1980-2003
Popular Names for this Generation	Veterans	Baby Boomers	Generation Xer's	The Nexters or Generation Y
What was the music of their early years?	▪ Swing ▪ Big Band ▪	▪ Rock 'n Roll ▪ Elvis ▪	▪ Disco ▪ Michael Jackson ▪	▪ Alternative Rap ▪ Backstreet Boys ▪

Birth Years	1922-1943	1943-1960	1960-1980	1980-2003
Popular Names for this Generation	Veterans	Baby Boomers	Generation Xer's	The Nexters or Generation Y
What defining events and trends ▪ ▪	The Great Depression ▪ ▪	Television ▪ ▪	Computers ▪ ▪	School Shootings ▪ ▪

Birth Years	1922-1943	1943-1960	1960-1980	1980-2003
Popular Names for this Generation	Veterans	Baby Boomers	Generation Xer's	The Nexters or Generation Y
Who were key people in the public eye during this period	<ul><li>Phil Donahue</li><li>Gloria Steinem</li><li></li></ul>	<ul><li>Bill Clinton</li><li>Oprah Winfrey</li><li></li></ul>	<ul><li>Brad Pitt</li><li>Michael Jordan</li><li></li></ul>	<ul><li>Kerri Strug</li><li>Tara Lipinski</li><li></li></ul>

Birth Years	1922-1943	1943-1960	1960-1980	1980-2003
Popular Names for this Generation	Veterans	Baby Boomers	Generation Xer's	The Nexters or Generation Y
Core Values	Dedication / Sacrifice • Conformity • Law and Order •	Optimism • Health and Wellness • Team Orientation •	Diversity *Techno-literacy • Fun •	Confidence • Street Smart • Optimism •

Adapted from Zemke, Ron, Raines, Claire, Filipczak, Bob, "Generations at Work"

Key Questions to Answer:

1. What impact did the influences you identified in Part One have on your level of awareness?

2. What impact did the influences you identified in Part Two have on your level of awareness?

3. Based upon the information collected in Part Two about each generation, what challenges would these observations pose for managing diversity?

4. How might your own "cultural software programming" add "benefits" and present "challenges" for working with others who are different from you in your personal and work life?

As you become more "self-aware, you must become aware of what you don't know about the lenses others use to perceive the world and what is "normal and natural to them. That requires knowledge and understanding.

Knowledge and Understanding

Knowledge and understanding are key areas that influence how we respond to workforce diversity according to Armida Mendez-Russell, co-author of the "Discovering Diversity Profile". Diversity knowledge is defined as "the extent to which an individual possesses information about others from diverse backgrounds and cultures". If developed properly, a person's knowledge base will proceed from notions of "stereotypes" due to cultural programming to a level of "information." When a manager operates with rudimentary awareness from basic cultural programming, stereotypes can develop because there is limited data.

With this limited data, managers tend to make generalizations about people. Many of these generalizations are based on stereotypes, that is, they operate on fixed images of groups of people that influence the ways the manager relates to individuals who are a part of that group. Stereotypes may possess some elements of fact in them, but each exaggerates and goes beyond the reality of fact. These generalizations may become "frozen" in the manager's mind. Even though he or she receives evidence to the contrary, they continue to hold on to these images as if they were fact.

As you build your knowledge base, you can progress to a more informed level of "information." At this stage in your development, by gathering factual data from books, magazines, videos, articles in the media, casual conversation, formal training, and from other sources, your images and viewpoints receive "enhanced programming." The more accurate information we have about others, the more likely it is that we will develop appropriate opinions, feelings, and behaviors. As you gather more information, it is possible to move your knowledge to a higher-level called "understanding".

"Understanding" can be defined as "the extent to which an individual comprehends how others feel and why they behave as they do." The basic level of understanding helps us to see that our personal reality is not the only reality. This level of understanding helps us apply our knowledge and information based to how it feels to interact with people who are different from ourselves. It clarifies who we are in comparison to other people's perceptions of us. This gives us a basis for contrasting our "cultural software programming" with someone who is different. It opens the door to the possibility that with our unique individual programming, two people can view the same situation differently and that "different is OK."

As your understanding grows, you are able to reach a level of "empathy" where you are able to show your ability to make connections with others on an emotional level. Managers who are empathic and possess mature levels of understanding can comprehend the emotions others are experiencing. They tend to recognize the reasons for the other person's point of view based upon their cultural programming. Empathy allows us to put ourselves in the other person's shoes, wear their glasses, trying to perceive "how it feels to look at the world through their lenses and walk their way." It makes us more flexible and less resistant, allowing us to become more sensitive to the differences among ourselves.

If we work on our knowledge and understanding to build our diversity maturity and effectiveness curve, we will ultimately get to a level of "acceptance," that is, we begin to respect and value the diverse characteristics and behaviors of others. This level of respect goes beyond simply "putting up" with others' differences or "being tolerated." Remember your observations in the "Tolerated versus Appreciated" exercise you completed earlier in Chapter 4? Few people, if any, simply want to be tolerated.

When you are a "respectful manager" in the diversity sense, you are able to grant full regard to the other person without compromise, based totally on the qualities they bring to the task at hand. Your views of the other person are not blemished or tarnished by negative cultural or racial characterizations. When you truly show respect for someone who is different from yourself, you see the value in having people contribute based upon on their background and culture. In fact, you appreciate their differences as added value to the organization. When managers create an atmosphere of respect for diversity, it creates trust, and in many cases, helps to stimulate improved productivity.

Behavioral Skills

As an effective diversity manager, at a behavioral level, you must be able to interact with others who are different from yourself. This requires that you understand your values, motives, and personal beliefs and their effect on what you do behaviorally. It requires that you do your own personal development work to take inventory of your strengths, weaknesses, and your level of sensitivity to the impact you have on others through your actions. It demands a level of accountability to develop the skills necessary to adjust our behavior while still maintaining your own identity, values, and beliefs. By knowing who you are and how your actions impact others, it clarifies your choices to select the most appropriate behavior.

A very skillful, diversity sensitive manager can effectively manage situations and successfully interact with people who may be different from themselves. When operating at this level, you are able to modify your behavior to meet the needs of the situation. Being effective in diverse workforce situations using interpersonal skills reflects an ability to be flexible in reacting to the ideas and opinions of others. It demonstrates respect and trust through cooperation, attentiveness and friendliness. This helps to create an

inclusive, high performing workplace that can make a
significant difference in organizational performance.

A beginning list of "Skills for Managing Diversity" was
published in the "Cultural Diversity at Work"
newsletter published by "The GilDeane Group" in
Seattle Washington. The list was developed
collaboratively with managers, readers, workshop
participants and the editors of the publication. This list
can be used to help you answer the question, "What am
I supposed to do differently?" It identifies the skills
according to seven categories. You will see areas in
which you may need to add skills to your repertoire.
These skills apply to a wide range of management
functions, including coaching, counseling, facilitating,
interviewing and conducting performance reviews. The
following interpersonal skills are important in
managing a diverse workforce:

Modify your Listening Skills:

- Recognize and adapt to the variety of listening behaviors you will encounter among diverse people.
- Listen for value-based cultural assumptions and expectations.
- Observe behavior and monitor your interpretations and meanings

Ask Necessary and Appropriate Questions:

- Learn about other views, work styles, assumptions and needs. Encourage others to do the same.
- Be comfortable in asking questions about the proper or preferred terminology, pronunciations, etc.
- Be comfortable in asking if you have caused offense, and find out how to correct and avoid it.
- Ask people to explain such things as goals, objectives, instructions and directions in order to ensure common understanding.

Shift Frame of Reference When Necessary:

- Demonstrate an understanding that perceptions are relative, and help others understand this

- Demonstrate empathy and understanding for
  other values, attitudes and beliefs; distinguish
  empathy from acceptance.
- Be flexible in your approach to situations;
  there are many ways of doing things.

Manage Conflict Constructively:

- Define the issue(s) in the conflict and focus on
  interests, not positions.
- Make an effort to understand other's
  perspectives.
- Demonstrate an understanding of different
  cultural assumptions about what conflict is and
  alternative ways of dealing with it.
- Develop a collaborative ("win-win") problem
  solving process.

Recognize Stereotypes and Generalizations:

- Be aware of and monitor your own
  stereotypes.
- Hold others accountable for their stereotypes.
- Learn to distinguish between individual
  differences and cultural differences.

Show Respect and Interest in the Other Person:

- Become acquainted with the geography, language, history, politics and customs of the native countries and cultures of those around you.
- Be aware that humor is perceived and handled in different ways by different cultural groups: Inappropriate humor may be perceived as insulting.
- When talking with non-fluent English speakers, speak clearly and avoid jargon and slang. Ask to make sure the person understand your meaning.

Be Approachable:

- Let others know, verbally and nonverbally, that you are willing to interact with them.
- Give cultural information freely when it is requested.
- Be open and accommodating to others' needs for gaining information; do not assume they know what you know.
- Learn to feel and exhibit comfort with groups and individuals different from yourself.

Developing skills to effectively manage a diverse workforce are no longer optional. In fact, they were required some time ago as our workforce demographic makeup changed. To be effective, managers must move through the continuum of becoming self-aware, improving their knowledge and understanding of diversity and translating that awareness, knowledge, and understand into a conscious decision to behave in a way that values the differences that employees bring to the workforce.

Setting the Tone for Valuing Diversity

Setting the tone for an environment that values diversity is a critical responsibility for any manager. Leading by example is the best method to let an employee see that you value diversity and encourage them to do so as well. Setting and living up to the behavioral standards for valuing diversity may not always be easy since our cultural programming can influence our basic response. However, if we let others know that we appreciate their differences and show that appreciation through our behavior and actions, workforce members begin to get the message that valuing diversity is truly a standard in which you believe and something they should do.

Even more importantly, as a manager, you must role model important decisions such as hiring, promotion, and allocating rewards in a way that is consistent with valuing diversity. Dr. R. Roosevelt Thomas described this familiar situation in a Harvard Business Review article.

"When I asked a white male middle manager how promotions were handled in his company, he said, 'You need leadership capability, bottom-line results, the ability to work with people, and compassion.' Then he paused and smiled. 'That's what they say. But down the hall, there's a guy we call Captain Kickass. He's

ruthless, mean-spirited, and he steps on people. That's
the behavior they really value. Forget what they say.'"

If behavior, which is the direct opposite of valuing
diversity, is allowed to go uncorrected or addressed,
employees get the message pretty clearly that this
"diversity and valuing differences" stuff is nothing but
"lip service". Managers must assess their behavior
often, ask for feedback, hold themselves accountable
and "walk the talk" if real change is to occur.

Some managers try to walk the talk by adhering to
the "Golden Rule", that is, "treating others as *you*
would like to be treated." It sounds good in theory,
however, this approach can unintentionally project your
own cultural programming related to perceptions,
values and beliefs of what is "right" and "wrong",
"good" and "bad", "appropriate" and "inappropriate"
onto others whose needs, values, and beliefs are
dramatically different. For example, in some cultures, it
is considered impolite or down right rude to bring

attention to yourself in a group meeting, yet some managers may not know that by recognizing a work team member in front of others, ringing their praises, could be embarrassing to them and to members of their culture who may be in attendance. The assumption that people want to be treated like you would want to be treated leads to "one size fits all thinking." It assumes that if you like it, others will like it too. Instead, it may be more effective to practice the "Platinum Rule", that is, "treat others as **_they_** want to be treated." This approach values what is needed from the other person's perspectives, values and beliefs.

To find out what others want, you can ask questions of them directly such as:

1. What do you want most from your job?
2. Under what conditions do you do your best work?
3. How would you like me to show recognition for your hard work?

4. How would you like to receive suggestions for improving your work?

5. What are your short and long-term career goals?

6. In what ways do you think people in our department, including yourself, are different from one another?

7. How do these differences affect our working together as a team?

8. How can and do these differences affect our overall productivity?

9. What policies and procedures inhibit you from doing your absolute best work?

10. What things am I doing that helps and hinders our work together as a team?

11. What biases do you perceive I reflect?

12. What suggestions do you have for me as a manager or team leader?

These are just a few questions to get you and your diverse work team on an inclusive path for performance.

From a behavioral standpoint, managers must also project a positive self-fulfilling prophecy with others that reflects trust, confidence and appreciation for the value they bring to the workplace. The implications of the self-fulfilling prophecy in the workplace are dramatic. Because of the stereotypical cultural programming we all have been raised with, we may unknowingly project self-fulfilling prophecies onto others that actually wind up occurring in the workplace.

For example, it may be assumed that traditional employees are competent and more effective workers and that employees from other groups may be less competent until proven otherwise. The manager's role is critical in this dynamic process because he or she has the authority to give or withhold rewards. If we assume that a person will fail, they often do – largely as a result of the negative climate, lower expectations, and impact on the individual's motivation level. When we truly believe that an employee is capable and our behavior is congruent with that assumption, employees often become motivated to show us that we are not wrong. As an effective manager of diversity, it is better to assume that people are competent and will succeed, until they prove otherwise. The self-fulfilling prophecy is particularly important with non-traditional employees because the traditional work environment has automatically assumed that individuals from these groups are less competent, thus putting them at an immediate disadvantage.

In summary, we know that developing competency to effectively manage diversity is continuous learning process. It requires self-awareness, knowledge and understanding and behavior changes that value others for who they are, not what we want them to be. To do this effectively, here are a few ideas to get you started:

- **Know your own culture (values, beliefs, assumptions).**
    - o Reflect on your early life experiences, and those significant emotional events that have shaped your value system and your beliefs and attitudes about those who are different from you. Answer the relevant questions such as what formative influences shaped your points of view-place of origin, family structure, socioeconomic status, religion, education and the like.
    - o Keep a journal. Carefully note your reactions to current world events and news reports, and describe and analyze your interactions with others.
    - o Enroll in courses that examine and discuss cultures, values, and beliefs

- **Know your own limitations (strengths and
  weaknesses).**

  o Request-and really listen to-feedback
     from multiple sources about your
     strengths and weaknesses. And be
     sure to get such feedback only from
     people you are sure will "tell it like it
     is" not from those who will merely
     tell you what you want to heat. In
     particular, try to get feedback from
     people who are from a different race
     or gender.

  o Seek out those experiences that will
     enable you to practice your strengths
     and shore up your weaknesses.

  o Change whatever you can about
     yourself, and accept whatever you
     can't, or won't. But above all, be very
     aware of the consequences, for better
     or worse, of changing or not
     changing.

- **Practice empathy with each other.**
  - Develop friendships and relationships with as many people form as many diverse backgrounds as you can, not only at work but outside of work as well.
  - Listen closely to the views of those friends and acquaintances and work hard to understand them, especially if these worldviews differ widely from your own.
  - Join organizations that expressly seek to advance the interests of different race and gender groups.
- **Respect other cultures.**
  - Cultivate friendships with people from as many cultures as possible.
  - Don't rush to judgment when it comes to areas of cultural difference. Values are not necessarily better or worse than one another, but can

> simply reflect a cherishing of our differences.

- o When judging others' cultural values and norms, refrain from using no other yardstick but your own.
- o Continually ask yourself whether you are making a value judgment about others, rather than recognizing that they simply may have different ways of reaching their goals.

- **Learn by interacting.**
  - o Join associations that deal specifically with the concerns of a particular race or gender.
  - o Pay close attention to the way others react to your behavior.
  - o When uncertain as to just what those reactions of others may mean, simply ask them and fully absorb their

responses without second guessing
them.

- **Strive to be nonjudgmental.**
    - o Try to understand the hidden
      dynamics of your interactions with
      others, rather than merely pretend that
      frictions don't exist.
    - o Remember that evolution has
      programmed our brains to make snap
      judgments; learn to work with that
      tendency, in order to rise above it.
    - o Remember that your own culture is
      only one standard, when it comes to
      assessing cultural norms and values.
    - o Acknowledge frankly that whenever
      we make snap judgments about an
      event or a person, it invariably does
      affect our next encounter with them.

- **Be aware of your stereotypes.**
  - Recognize that while stereotyping is normal, it is dangerous. And understand that while the brain and mind stereotype, we have the opportunity to frankly acknowledge that fact and prevent it from showing up in our behavior.
  - Develop relationships with people of other racial or ethnic groups, and any of the other gender.
  - Enter freely and openly into learning situations where stereotypes are openly identified and confronted.
  - Ask people you trust to gently challenge you, if they believe you have used a stereotype in making a judgment.

- **Learn how to communicate effectively and
  compassionately.**
  - o Practice speaking directly and
    candidly, and clearly, but also
    tactfully and compassionately.
  - o Listen actively; paraphrase what the
    other person has said and then ask
    him or her whether your paraphrase is
    an accurate version of what he or she
    was trying to convey.
  - o Continually check and recheck your
    perceptions, asking yourself whether
    your interpretations of behavior and
    nonverbal signals have been valid.

- **Listen closely, and observe carefully.**
  - o Ask probing questions to help you
    distinguish between what someone
    actually has said or done and your
    own reactions to or judgments about
    it.

- o Ask those you trust to gently
  challenge you on those occasions
  when you seemed to be listening, but
  really were not.
- o Consider talking less and thinking
  and listening more.
- o Develop your powers of observation,
  by taking part in workshops where
  trained facilitators will give you
  immediate feedback as to your
  awareness or lack of it.
- o Enter into a no-holds-barred
  discussion about work situations,
  with people you trust of both genders,
  and of different racial and ethnic
  backgrounds.

- **Strive to relate meaningfully to those you
  perceive as "different".**
    - o Recognize that the entire organization
      must continually strive to understand,

value, respect, and appreciate
differences, if the organization is to
be more competitive.

o Understand that complementary skills
and strengths promote a higher level
of quality in terms of tasks, products
and relationships

- **Be flexible; learn how to adapt.**

  o Spending some time with people
  from diverse cultures, both at and
  outside of work.

  o Consciously seeking out knowledge
  and experience relating to different
  cultures and people to expand your
  own range of options and choices.

  o Reading publications that express
  viewpoints differing from your own.

- Traveling to experience other peoples cultures in their surroundings rather than your own.

- **Adjust yourself according to people's reactions.**
  - Solicit feedback from as many different sources as possible.
  - Practice adjusting your behavior in response to that feedback, then request more feedback on your adjustments.

- **Learn how to live with ambiguity.**
  - Seek out situations, both at work and outside of work, that induce discomfort; then find ways of raising your comfort level.
  - Solicit guidance as to the appropriate behavior, when you find yourself in ambiguous circumstances.

- **Be as consistent as you can be, without becoming inflexible.**
  - Soliciting feedback from a variety of people at work and outside of work who have had a chance to observe you with opportunities to deal with unfamiliar situations (Fernandez, 1999).

This chapter has presented you with some tools and techniques to help you develop competencies for effectively managing diversity. If you and your organization strives to be effective in our global marketplace, it is imperative that you maintain personal and system-wide accountability for your awareness, knowledge and actions. Your individual success and the organization's success depend on it!

References

Carnevale, Anthony Patrick, Kogod, Kanu S., Tools and Activities for a Diverse Work Force, McGraw-Hill, Inc, New York, 1996. Contributing article by Gardenswartz, Lee, Rowe, Anita "Management Development Diversity Needs Analysis: Awareness, Knowledge, and Skills", p. 43

Carnevale, Anthony Patrick, Kogod, Kanu S., Tools and Activities for a Diverse Work Force, McGraw-Hill, Inc, New York, 1996. Contributing article by Deane, Barbara, The GilDeane Group, Seattle, WA, "Skills for Managing Diverse People: Making a List , p. 228-231

Fernandez, John P, "Race, Gender & Rhetoric", McGraw-Hill, New York, 1999.

Hubbard, Edward E., "Techniques for Managing a
Diverse Workforce", Global Insights Publishing,
Petaluma, CA, 2002.

Rasmussen, Tina, The ASTD Trainer's
Sourcebook: Diversity, McGraw-Hill, New York, 1996.

Zemke, Ron, Raines, Claire, Filipczak, Bob,
Generations at Work, AMACOM, New York, 2000.

Chapter Six: Workplace Applications

Introduction

Diversity is a challenge that has the potential to be either a positive or a negative influence on an organization. Ignoring the fact that diversity exists and treating all people as if there are no differences between them will grossly underutilize a critical asset of the organization. "Diversity is not only about 'representation', it about 'utilization'!" "Its not about counting heads, but making heads count!" In order for diversity to have a positive effect, a manager's awareness, knowledge, understanding, and behavior must be combined to create specific actions to capitalize on and leverage the power of diversity. Otherwise, this valuable resource will go untapped.

Diversity can be leveraged in a wide variety of areas throughout the organization. In this chapter, we will examine how diversity strategies can be applied to:

- Recruitment / Selection
- Employee Retention and Development
- Team Building
- Customer Service
- Improving Market Share

Recruitment / Selection

Recruitment and selection is often the first place organizations will start when building a diverse work environment. Oftentimes however, many organizations demonstrate only a superficial commitment to diversity in spite of the demographic and other evidence to the contrary. A common refrain heard by many goes something like this: "if only we could find some truly

qualified women and minorities, we would be happy to
hire them. Those folks don't seem to be interested in
the type of work we do in our industry. If you find
some, we'll hire them."

In reality, this type of statement at best, is an
unfounded assertion and at its worst, reflects another
form of racism and sexism that stems from cultural
programming that has effectively gone unchallenged.
Qualified women and minorities are certainly out there
if the work environment and the job offers are right.
There's no secret in finding them, however,
organizations need to rely on diverse recruitment
people and diverse approaches to attract and retain a
"diverse" workforce. Its simply a matter of committing
the organization to developing systematic, objective,
rational, and fair recruiting strategies, implementing
those strategies aggressively, and fostering an team
environment that treats people fairly, regardless of their
differences.

The current changing landscape of American demographics, both native and foreign born reflects a labor pool that comprises a large population of educated, capable people from diverse backgrounds, especially in the high-tech and service-based industries. Any U.S. organization that desires to stay competitive for now and in the future is going to have to find, recruit, and retain the best employees, regardless of their diverse backgrounds. Too often, recruiters and their organizations evaluate new recruits solely on the basis of how they "fit" the organization's culture, which is somewhat antiquated in today's hiring practices and requirements (today, many organizations try avoid hiring in their own image). Many of these interviews are unstructured and haphazard; the interviewers are often poorly trained in how to conduct a "culture-fair", objective interview. And, there are very few metrics and incentives that encourage the interviewers to make certain they obtain a diverse candidate pool.

To be effective, recruiters and their organizations should look at an employee's intellectual, technical, and professional skills and at their desire, their understanding of their personal culture, their strengths and weaknesses, their emotional intelligence, their ability to be empathetic, and their willingness to accept and value different race, ethnic, and gender groups. Recruiters, interviewers and hiring managers need effective tools to help them make good decisions regarding the best person for the job given "all" of the human resources available without the hindrance of bias. The following steps can be helpful in avoiding race and gender bias in the recruitment and hiring process:

Step to Avoid Race and Gender Bias	
Step	**Activity**
1	**Develop specific selection criteria.** It is essential to develop specific hiring criteria,

	and to make sure that all of the interviewers and hiring managers make use of them.
2	**Develop specific instruments to measure the criteria.** Everyone in the interviewing and hiring process should be using them. A matrix usually works well as a summary tool. List the candidates down the left side and the criteria across the top row. For each cell created, enter the candidate's response on each criterion listed. In this way you can compare their responses against the same criteria.
3	**Train Interviewers.** Interviewers need to go through their own self-analysis to examine their own culture, norms, values, emotional intelligence, racial and gender attitudes, and the like. They should go through the recruitment process, just like any other new job candidate. And they should receive feedback from recruits about their skills.

4	**Have Diverse Interviewers.** Because of our natural tendency to hire people like ourselves, it is crucial that women and minorities are recruiters and interviewers.
5	**Use a Team Approach.** All parties to the process should meet as a team, to review candidates and to arrive at a team decision.
6	**Evaluate the Recruiters.** Recruiters should be evaluated in terms of their number of hires as well as of the race and gender, type of positions, and the success or failure of their recruits.

Developing College Connections

A number of organizations have recognized that soon, we will experience a "birth dearth" period based upon our census data. That is, due to the lack of births in recent years, there will be a 27.9% reduction in the talent available for work over an 18-year period. During that 18-year period, there will be a 7-year "drought" period. Because of this and other labor shortage issues, more and more organizations are acknowledging their need for a systematic, year-round college relations program that can begin to woo candidates from all backgrounds when they are just starting their educational careers. The following are some key elements of an effective college relations program:

1. Evaluate and select a limited number of specific schools that have a good track record in terms of producing diverse talent that matches your organization's present and future needs, especially those colleges that have high populations of each targeted demographic group.

2. Dedicate to each college a diverse team headed by a senior officer.

3. Train team members in their roles, and include diversity and multicultural interviewing training on an ongoing basis.

4. Maintain a year-round presence at the college; don't just show up at recruitment time, when most likely the best candidates already have been snapped up anyway.

5. Evaluate the teams in terms of their success or failure in attracting women and minority candidates.

6. Create and review your recruitment success metrics and publish the results to the rest of the organization.

When your diverse recruitment teams are planning "on-campus" strategies to create an effective approach, here's a few actions they can take to improve their hit rate:

On-Campus Strategies Checklist	
☑	**Activity**
	Have formal and informal lunches and dinners with key students, faculty members and administrators.
	Seek out and develop relationships with various students clubs and professional associations such as Historically Black Colleges and Universities (HBCU), Hispanic Association of Colleges and Universities (HACU), Catalyst (Women's Organization), INROADS (Inner City and Youth Development Organization), and others; and don't forget the organizations on campus that are devoted to meeting the needs of part-time, returning, and evening students.
	Volunteer to personally give lectures and conduct classes, and/or recruit some suitable

	employees who are not on the team to help you out in this regard.
	Support student activities, and provide financial or in-kind help as part of your organization's community development effort. This will help to bolster the organization's image on campus.
	Provide year-round, ongoing internships for students, and get the jump on other organizations by letting them begin in their senior year of high school.
	Provide a "Step Ahead" program for students -- where students work in the organization during their summer vacation and short periods of time (when school is out during other periods). Be sure that they get real experience on projects of substance, not just

	used as an extra pair of hands in the mailroom. Have their projects end with a written or oral report. This allows them to summarize what they learned and demonstrate their on-the-job learning.

It is also critical to have strategies to recruit seasoned employees to fill positions at all levels. Organizations can't afford to overlook the recruitment of experienced employees to fulfill key strategic positions within the organization. Here are just a few ideas to get you started:

- Develop contacts with stakeholders from diverse backgrounds.
- Develop relationships with local and national religious, professional, political, and social organizations whose focus is people from diverse groups.

- Locate and develop relationships with
  recruitment firms dedicated to diverse groups.
- Develop a recruitment directory that contains
  listings for people from women and minority
  search firms, colleges and universities,
  sororities, fraternities, professional and
  political associations, community
  organizations, publications to advertise in, and
  vocational and technical schools.
- Remember, this is not about "Quotas". It is
  about finding the person who is "best
  qualified" for the job given "all" of the talent
  pools available.

When you talk with diverse groups during the
recruiting process, don't be surprised if they are
skeptical. Based on different experiences, they may
want to "check out" the organization to see if it is
diversity-friendly. They may ask questions such as the
following which you must be prepared to answer or

demonstrate in your behavior during the recruitment process:

☑	Diversity-Friendly Environment Question Check/Preparation List
	Activity
	What is the level of women and minorities in senior positions?
	What is the company's philosophy of and commitment to developing women and minorities?
	What is the level of commitment of the organization to diversity and Affirmative Action?
	How has the organization handled charges of discrimination in the past?
	How sensitive, aware, and comfortable are interviewers with candidates of diverse backgrounds?

	How honest, straightforward, and candid are interviewers during the recruitment process?
	The extent to which the company keeps to the commitments it makes throughout the recruitment process.
	How do other women and minorities view the organization?
	How the community perceives the organization's reputation and involvement.
	What's the organization's attitude regarding balancing work and personal life?

Recruiting for a highly successful diverse workforce involves developing a vision for building and supporting a diverse workforce in your organization. This includes considering how you recruit both internally and externally.

Internal Recruiting

Left on its own, internal recruiting usually occurs without much thought given to issues of utilizing the diversity that exists within the organization unless there is a clear commitment to building and supporting a diverse work environment. There often seems to be a disproportionate number of people of color, women, people with disabilities, etc., in front-line worker positions versus management positions. There are both pros and cons to internal recruiting.

On the one hand, promoting from within is very cost effective and can boost morale by letting employees know that hard work does pay off in opportunities for growth and development. One of the downsides of internal recruiting is that your organization can miss the opportunity to bring in fresh new talent with new perspectives and approaches. Another downside of internal recruiting is that the organization can become wrapped up in its' own organizational programming that it stagnates due to excessive inbreeding of ideas and process. An inbred organization may approach problem solving, and operational processes with tunnel vision. In addition, any new ideas that suggest changes and innovation may meet head on with resistance.

An effective internal recruiting process will take into account internal resources such as:

- **Promotions** – Examining your leadership development, specialized technical, and general managerial programs to locate candidates. This is a good place to assess whether or not your diversity efforts are working. Conduct a demographic analysis of the make up of these groups. Do they include women and minorities, or people who are a part of an underrepresented group? How often have these programs graduated someone who is a part of a diverse group? What support

programs have been put in place to help ensure
a successful start?

- **Transfers** – "Job shadowing" opportunities
  can enhance learning and impact career
  choices. When this is done however, it is
  critical to make certain the climate the
  transferee will experience is a positive one.
  The transfer group may need some diversity
  training before they are left to operate on their
  own.

- **Work Teams** – Work teams need diversity
  training as well. Simply because a team
  contains members with diverse backgrounds
  does not make them effective. Remember,
  diversity is about "utilization" not
  "representation". These teams can be another
  source of talent.

- **Committee** – Reviewing members who are a
  part of special committees can also be a source
  of possible talent for growth. This assumes
  that the process for accessing these committees

is open to a variety of members from diverse backgrounds. In many cases, selection to participate on these committees can be tantamount to promotion and even succession. In some organizations, women and minorities rarely get nominated as part of the committee selection process.

External Recruiting

External recruiting is often well organized, having a systematic and consistent approach. Many organizations use the same resources to draw new employees year after year. The unspoken belief may be "if it's not broken, why fix it?" The flaw in this type of thinking is that if you don't seek out new resources, you will not diversify your applicant pool. The challenge here is to expand your horizons and seek out additional and perhaps non-traditional sources of applicants.

As with internal recruiting, there are both pros and cons to external recruiting. If your organization is actively seeking a skill set that is not available internally, it is to your benefit to look outside. Also, if you are trying to improve your organization's diversity mixture, there is a larger pool of candidates outside. However, keep in mind that there are consequences involved. Employees who do not get promotional opportunities are left wondering: "Why not me?" They may not see the skill and qualification differences being brought in from the outside. This is made worse when this same employee is asked to show the new person how things should operate. Loss of morale, loyalty, and satisfaction can be the result of this action.

Be sure to make use some of the following recruiting channels that involve traditional and non-traditional sources as well as create specialized lists of your own:

- Chamber of Commerce
- Church Activities
- Sporting Events
- Community Organizations
- Family and Friends of Diverse Groups (employee referrals)
- Career Days
- Disabled Student Services
- Corporate Sponsored Events that are Diversity Focused
- Service providers that have access to diverse groups
- Using Multi-cultured Media Advertisements
- Etc.

Potential employees will usually get their first look at the organization based upon your recruitment efforts and media exposure. It is one of the best places to start to apply your skills to build a diverse work environment.

Employee Retention and Development

In addition to recruiting a diverse workforce, there must be processes in place to retain and develop them. The ability to retain the diverse work group once recruited is a critical management competency. It helps to avoid "human capital depletion" and "revolving-door impact." Some organizations do a wonderful job setting up systems to recruit diverse employees only to lose them 12-18 months later in voluntary turnover (human capital depletion). This often occurs because there is little thought given to retaining them once they are inside the organization. If this happens, they show up in the "revolving-door" statistics (poor survival rate).

Making a commitment to diversity and inclusion means more than striving for immediate results such as improved demographics. Employees must feel welcomed and supported. They need to know that the organization has systems, processes and people in place

to help give them the best possible chance for success
and allow them to build an invigorating career.

Training programs are one form of development,
however training programs alone are not enough to
keep employee for the long run. Employee retention
and development must be a complete, comprehensive
system, which includes processes, and systems such as:

- Coaching and Counseling
- Career Planning
- Mentoring
- Succession Planning
- Performance Rating Equity Analysis
- Compensation Equity Analysis
- Diversity-friendly policies and procedures
- Etc.

The following processes and techniques can be
used to improve employee retention and development:

Employee Retention and Development Idea List	
☑	**Activity**
	Create a **"pre-recruitment training"** program designed to tackle issues concerning lack of information about available jobs, diverse candidate's lack of confidence, poor interview skills, etc.
	Review job vacancies to make certain that "individual preferences" **ARE NOT** being substituted for "real job requirements".
	Solicit ideas from recent hires and current employees who represent diverse groups regarding potential sources of candidates for hiring slates.
	Help sponsor an internship for women, people of color, and other underrepresented

☑	**Employee Retention and Development Idea List**
	Activity
	groups (age, people with disabilities, protected classes, etc.)
	Attend or sponsor Career Fairs or "recruiting rallies" focused on Women and People of Color and serve as an interviewer. Offer development seminars covering different subjects such as "Developing Professional Selling Skills, Interviewing Skills, Etiquette, Benefits—your hidden paycheck, and diversity in the workplace.
	Review all slates for hires, promotions, and laterals to ensure their diversity balance.
	Commit a full-time resource to address recruitment for women and people of color.

☑	Employee Retention and Development Idea List
	Activity
	Provide and obtain timely and specific performance feedback.
	Create methods to analyze the reasons for losses of women and people of color by level as given by employees and their managers. Check for themes and patterns to take corrective action.
	If women and/or people of color have voluntarily left the organization, ***make certain Exit Interviews are conducted prior to their departure and six months later.*** If possible, the exit interviews should be conducted by an external third party. The later time period and third party interviews reduce inhibitions to

☑	**Employee Retention and Development Idea List**
	Activity
	criticize an ex-employer for fear of reprisal.
	Create assessments e.g., targeted survey, and focus groups, to determine if women and people of color feel their talents, skills and abilities are underutilized.
	Create an assessment e.g., targeted survey, and focus groups, to determine if women and people of color feel they have been given sufficient responsibility and authority to make decisions within their current organization.
	Conduct mentoring programs for high potential women and minorities. Also use "reverse mentoring", that is having mentors who are working with others who are different

Employee Retention and Development Idea List	
☑	**Activity**
	from themselves.
	Assign a "Peer-Coach" to new hires. A "Peer-Coach" is a person who is available to a new hire to answer questions, help them navigate the culture and systems of the organization, introduce them to others and help bridge their transition to the workplace.
	Creating skill development and cross-training opportunities like "job-sharing" or placing diverse employees in charge while you are on vacation or on special assignment for your own development.

One of the primary goals of retention and development processes is to develop employees such that they can do their absolute personal best work and will want to remain with the organization to build a career. It becomes expensive when this is not done. For those looking for hard numbers to support the value of diversity, an obvious place to start looking is to examine the organization's turnover and productivity numbers. Each year, organizations spend millions of dollars recruiting and training employees. When the employee experiences a poor, unwelcoming work environment, they get the message pretty clearly that "it may be a nice place to train, but you wouldn't want to work here". So they don't, they usually wind up leaving the organization. In these cases, diverse workforce turnover can become a serious problem. As a result, the organization pays the price of turnover that is on average 1.5 times the salary of the person who leaves, and that's just to get them in the door! This represents a poor return on investment for the organization.

Even when turnover is relatively small, the unwillingness of an organization to step up to the issue of valuing diversity can lower morale and productivity. In the competitive business environment of today, organizations simply cannot afford to sacrifice any level of productivity. Even marginal declines in productivity can put an organization in serious jeopardy of losing some portion of their competitive advantage (Loden, 1996).

The approaches shown here are just are just a few examples of techniques you can use to help you manage and improve the retention of your diverse workforce.

Team Building

One of the greatest opportunities for the organization's use of diversity in a business improvement context is the ability maximize the utilization of diverse work teams. As mentioned earlier, this is not an automatic occurrence simply because you put people who are different in the same room. Managers must help the group go through a distinct process of personal and group identity change if the value they bring to the organization will be realized.

First, you must help team members understand the differences that each member brings to the team. As a team member, they will meet and constantly work with others whose culture may differ considerably from their own. Think about it, when team members meet for the first time, they will typically base their impressions on their physical appearance, facial features, skin color, hair, stature, dress, mannerisms, voice tone, etc. However, after working together, they have the opportunity to learn about each other at a deeper level, and not be influenced by their first impressions only. They may have notice different behaviors that seemed awkward and/or peculiar or difficult to understand. They may often need your help in utilizing your knowledge (and the development of their own) of cultural differences to make them more comfortable. In essence, you will help them bridge the cultural differences gap to construct a foundation for future learning. Selma G. Myers has developed a *"Team Development Model"* which suggests that although traditional teams will go through these five stages, diverse workgroups go through these stages differently and will deal with issues that may not come up or be as unsettling in homogeneous groups (Myers, 1996):

Driving Stage: This stage involves the team in focusing on its mission, goals, priorities, and guidelines. However, while some cultural groups are comfortable in a structured environment, other groups may not be. When you add dynamics such as language (i.e., English is not the first language of some of the members and they find it difficult to comprehend), different values around time, variations in norms regarding group interaction, viewpoints on authority, it changes the speed with which the group can move

forward and can affect their development if it is not
handled well.

Strive Stage: This stage involves moving ahead
with full understanding and agreement on roles and
responsibilities. However, some cultural groups have
great interest in gaining more responsibility, while
others are not as open to taking on responsibility
without formal support such as rank, age, etc. Some
individuals may be very open to the concept of change
while others are satisfied with the status quo.

Thrive Stage: This stage involves rapid growth
involving peer feedback, conflict management, and
decision-making. However, various cultural groups
may have different approaches to communication and
conflict, and reach decisions in a number of different
ways. For example, certain cultures value directness
and frankness in interpersonal communication, while
others place a high value on subtlety in their
communication style.

Arrive Stage: This stage involves peak performance, where all the factors are in sync. Finally, the team has arrived when all members have been recognized, appreciated, accepted, encouraged, and acknowledged in a way that is consistent with their cultural, for the strengths they bring to the team.

Revive Stage: This stage involves regaining peak performance when slippage in team performance occurs, when the team memberships changes, or when the team's mandate or purpose has changed. At this stage, the interaction between members of the diverse team needs to be reexamined. Blaming, without recognizing cultural differences, is counterproductive. When knowledge of cultural differences is used effectively, team members remain open-minded, and motivated and support each other to attain peak performance again.

In order for diverse work teams to be effective the following characteristics must be in place:

Effective Diversity Work Team Characteristics	
☑	**Key Components**
	A Strong Mission or Purpose – Teams may disagree about many things and have vigorous disputes with each other, however, when they have an overarching mission or purpose that is strong, compelling and transcends cultural barriers (such as building an inclusive work environment that work for all of us), the team finds a way to work together. Diverse work teams want to know that they have a role to play that is valued and that they have a stake in the outcome.
	A Clear Defined Performance Outcome – No mater what type of team you have (diverse or traditional), it is critical that the members of the team have a clear and well-defined performance outcome that creates a "line-of-

Effective Diversity Work Team Characteristics

☑	Key Components
	sight" understanding of their work and how it add value to the organization. The team's performance outcome(s) must be measurable, specific, and time-bound for which the team can be held accountable. It is difficult to drum up excitement and support for an outcome that is ill defined.
	An Understanding of Different Cultural Norms and their Impact on Team Communication, Problem-Solving, and Conflict – United States cultural norms tend to favor analytical over intuitive problem solving and favor directness over avoidance in conflict management. This is certainly not the case in other cultures and in a diverse team; the lack of sensitivity to these kinds of issues can spell disaster and breed dysfunction. In some non-

	Effective Diversity Work Team Characteristics
☑	**Key Components**
	U.S. based cultures, ethnic groups prize harmonious interactions when dealing with differences and utilize communication strategies that keep the conversations purposely vague and indirect. Understanding these norms is critical to a diverse work team's functioning at both a personal and group level. If synergy is to develop, the team and its leader must be knowledgeable and skilled in the use of "cultural frames of reference" to help create team solutions.
	A Set of Shared Values the Clearly Articulate Demonstrations of Dignity and Respect – Everyone wants to be valued and treated with respect and dignity. What is unclear is the way every culture wants to be valued and

Effective Diversity Work Team Characteristics

☑	**Key Components**
	respected, and the ways that show they have been treated with dignity. What measures should be used? One of the early exercises in the team's development (in the Driving Stage) should focus on identifying the elements that constitute a respectful way for the team to operate. We certainly are aware of the costs if this is not done. Teams disintegrate and become maladaptive groups or worse yet, poorly focused and frustrated individuals.
	A Cultivation of Different Points of View – Diverse work teams deal with their diversity much more easily and flexibly when they embrace differences by following the principle of "no fewer than three points of view." What this rule does is instill the belief that there is no

	Effective Diversity Work Team Characteristics
☑	**Key Components**
	best way and that the more options you have, the better your potential solutions are. Just legalizing the notion that things aren't "either-or" sets up a norm and value in the team that identifying different approaches from different perspectives, and judging them on their value to the stated need opens up everyone thinking to exploration.
	A Willingness to Do What It Takes To Get the Job Done – A key ingredient for excellence in the team is the team member's commitment to being accountable for his or her assigned tasks and working with others interactively and cooperatively until the job is done. Team members make certain that all members cross the finish line together, handling obstacles and providing support as needed.

The Executive's Pocket Coach to Diversity and
Inclusion Management

Effective Diversity Work Team Characteristics	
☑	**Key Components**
	Contribution is measured by what the team is able to accomplish and improved performance is assessed by how well the team can analyze itself and collectively implement changes and perform. The task does not go unfinished, nor does a member get left behind.
	Loyalty and Devotion to the Team Experience – Loyalty, and particularly devotion, are strong words and rarely mentioned as a necessity when discussing team performance. Nevertheless, they are important because they imply passion and energy, not just run-of-the-mill work. It is possible to accomplish a task without true devotion to the whole experience; however, it may leave a lot to be desired. For some cultures, this level of

Effective Diversity Work Team Characteristics	
☑	**Key Components**
	passion and devotion to the outcome is a driving force.
	A Desire for Individual and Collective Growth – Part of the intrigue and frustration of a diverse work team process is that you have to merge your skills, competencies, ideas, values, and priorities with others. Figuring out how to do that well is a complex process that requires tenacity. Although a diverse work team members' skills and knowledge may be complementary and not necessarily conflicting, aligning priorities, making decisions, and solving problems frequently exposes areas of friction in the team. The individual and exponential growth of the team and its members will depend on its ability to work through these

Effective Diversity Work Team Characteristics

☑	Key Components
	"frictional moments of truth." Some teams are nearly pushed to the breaking point when these frictional moments occur. It is what they do in these moments, along with their cultural knowledge base and processes agreed to ahead of time, which determine if the team truly learns from the situation and acquires the skills needed to handle any other present or future conflicts. This is an on-going competency building process that if mastered, creates a significant operational and competitive advantage for the organization.
	An Openness to New Experiences and Processes, Both Interpersonal and Problem Solving – Learning can't enter through a closed mind. Being a life-long learner and open to new

☑	**Effective Diversity Work Team Characteristics**
	Key Components
	experiences goes a long way towards effectively working with and accepting others who are different. There is a saying that states once your mind is stretched with a new idea, it never goes back to the same shape. You take that knowledge with you. Diverse work teams, if properly managed, can allow all members of the team to grow and develop.
	Shared Laughter and Humor as an Integral Part of the Team Experience – While having fun as teammates in the process of accomplishing a task is not absolutely necessary, it adds immeasurably to the experience of working together. In fact, it is an important determinant in creating more tenacity and follow-through in meeting the team's

☑	**Effective Diversity Work Team Characteristics**
	Key Components
	performance objectives. Oftentimes, teams will notice how much their quality and productivity was enhanced, not sacrificed, through their laughter and that it made the team experience one they wanted to repeat.

Customer Service and Improving Market Share

When it comes to addressing issues of diversity's link to the financial bottom-line, one of the most compelling yet underused and least leveraged arguments is diversity's link and connection to customer service and satisfaction, both internal and external customers. Unfortunately, managers and even some diversity practitioners have not gotten this connection. Some that do get it, do not try to help their organization see this connection. The connection appears to be pretty straightforward.

If an organization does not foster a culture of understanding, respect, and cooperation, the ability of the workforce can be severely limited in effectively interacting with the diverse customers of the organization. Often, you hear organizations talking about their strategies to stay close to and focus on the customer, however, how comforting can it be to know that there is a high probability that your employees are marketing to, selling to, and interacting with your customers based upon outdated assumptions, personal biases, inaccurate stereotypes and disrespectful behaviors due to their cultural programming? If the organization has a high incidence of internal harassment complaints, can it feel confident that this is not a customer service issue too? If employees are uncomfortable dealing with their openly gay co-workers, are they likely to be effective and respectful

when dealing with customers or clients who are open
about their sexual orientation? In addition, are they
likely to aggressively go after important, strategic
business opportunities with this group or any group
they may have a bias against?

Whether sanctioned by the organization or not,
discriminatory practices are always costly. While some
may not lead to multi-million dollar lawsuits, they
tarnish the image and brand reputation of an
organization in the eyes of customers, investors, and
potential employees. It can lead to lost sales, boycotts,
and legal judgments that cost the organization millions
of dollars in lost revenues, management and legal costs
and the like.

Organizations intent on leveraging diversity in
their marketplace must also understand the particular
consumer preferences of their diverse customers. Major
corporations such as Nike, Ford, McDonalds, Coke, and
others are going all out to win over free-spending ethnic

consumers, recruiting minority marketing experts who
speak each group's language and know their customs.
Mass marketing is a relic of the past when America was
a cultural melting pot. Today, you need a different
message to suit the taste of each group. With data based
marketing techniques becoming more sophisticated,
diverse market segments are easier to identify. Once
identified, it is possible to appeal to many segments in
separate and distinct ways, provided the organization
does its homework to develop a depth of knowledge on
each targeted group build relationships with them as
customers based upon their way they want to be treated
and "sold to". In addition, if internally, you have to
"sell your work" to internal customers who are different
from yourself, your effectiveness will be determined by
your ability to communicate across differences. No
matter who's the customer, the more knowledge you
acquire about the customer or client, the more chances
of your success in customizing and personalizing an
approach that meets that customers' needs.

In many cases, effectively selling to diverse markets will require identifying the obstacles that stand in the way of the organization building effective cross-cultural relationships with it customers. The organization's characteristics and the customer's unique background will determine what obstacles need to be overcome and their correct strategies to do so. If not done well, there are a number of disastrous consequences that can be created for failing to take the time to know your market. Here are just a few, well-publicized examples:

- In Hong Kong, a car rental company unsuccessfully attempted to promote itself by giving away green hats, The company was unaware of the Chinese superstition that if a man wears a green hat, his wife is cheating on him!

- A manufacturer of golf balls failed in a marketing effort in Japan. They were unaware that in Japan, there are negative connotations associated with the number four and with items grouped in four. The manufacturer here failed to get acquainted with its market, and by doing so failed to respect a cultural difference.

According to Fernandez, there are seven obstacles to cross-cultural marketing relationships and seven steps to do it effectively. Obstacles include the following:

Seven Obstacles To Cross-Cultural Marketing Relationships	
	Obstacles
1	Assuming that the entire target market segment is homogeneous; that is, assuming that all members of that market have identical values, beliefs, assumptions, preferences, wants, and needs.
2	Conducting little or no research into the wants, needs, and culture of the targeted

Seven Obstacles To Cross-Cultural Marketing Relationships	
Obstacles	
	segment, but instead merely falling back on gut feeling and stereotypes.
3	Erroneously believing that one can reach a targeted market segment through only one marketing method; e.g., assuming that all Hispanics can be reached through television, when in fact Spanish-language radio may be the more effective method.
4	Erroneously believing that a mass marketing strategy such as advertising can be quickly and painlessly adapted to a target market merely by translating it into that target market's preferred language.
5	Creating advertisements that are out of synch with the mood, values, and/or culture of

Seven Obstacles To Cross-Cultural Marketing Relationships	
	Obstacles
	the target market.
6	Placing advertisements only in mass-market publications rather than also utilizing publications geared directly towards the target market.
7	Blindly and expensively developing new products and services, on the basis of an unexamined assumption that the current product and service mix does not meet the targeted segment's needs and wants.

If these obstacles are to be overcome, he states a combination of internally and externally focused initiatives will have to be undertaken. In combination, these initiatives will help support the development of a target market strategy able to deliver value plus products an services over the short and long runs.

Seven Steps Towards an Effective Target Market Strategy	
Steps	**Key Strategies**
1	Understand your own and your organization's culture.
2	Understand the target market's culture.
3	Identify key stakeholder groups.
4	Develop relationships based upon trust and respect; become a proactive community citizen
5	Identify market segment needs, preference, and expectations through a variety of methods, such as interviews and focus groups.
6	Develop products, services, and delivery mechanisms that will deliver value-plus products to customers.
7	Continually check up on your progress, and ask members of the target market to provide you with ongoing feedback.

An example will help us envision how the use of these steps can help improve your marketplace effectiveness. To illustrate step 2: Understand the target market's culture, we will examine a situation from Southern New England Telephone.

"Southern New England Telephone took the time to understand why its Hispanic accounts had a much higher delinquency rate than its other accounts. What it discovered was that many aspects of Hispanic culture were directly clashing with its customer service system. For example, the average Hispanic customers felt a need to develop rapport with a customer service representative before he or she is comfortable getting down to business; the abrupt style that SNET had taught its reps caused many Hispanics to feel alienated, and hesitant to call the company to work out a problem. SNET also found that their policy of not accepting third-party checks or cash payments made it difficult for Hispanic customers to pay their bills, and that using only English on their bills made it difficult for many

Hispanic customers to understand them. Therefore, you can see how, by simply making an effort to get to know the culture and needs of their Hispanic customers, SNET was able to significantly lower its delinquency rates."

Another example involves General Motors.

"In 1996, General Motors won a $1 billion automotive deal with China, in large part because back in 1986 it had hired a very prominent, American-born Chinese woman who was well connected in China. In addition, they had a company support (affinity) group for Asians. Therefore, the company's knowledge of China and its culture, and some key contacts, gave GM a leg up over the other major car manufacturers who were pursuing the same contract."

Still, another example:

"Acknowledging that its products weren't selling well in Asia, Bausch & Lomb turned to its Asian employees for guidance. Their inquires led them to the discovery that Bausch & Lomb glasses weren't fitting Asian people properly. Sales rose, once the company had modified its glasses for its Asian markets.

As these examples and this chapter illustrates, there are a wide variety of organizational applications that support the notion that diversity is a key strategic business issue. It involves utilization of diverse workforce asset beyond mere representation. Whether its recruitment and selection, employee retention and development, team building, or customer service or improving market share, a manager's job is to utilize diversity for the optimal performance of the organization and its employees.

References

Fernandez, John P, "Race, Gender & Rhetoric",
McGraw-Hill, New York, 1999.

Hubbard, Edward E., "Techniques for Managing a
Diverse Workforce", Global Insights Publishing,
Petaluma, CA, 2002.

Loden, Marilyn, Implementing Diversity, Irwin,
Chicago, Illinois, 1996.

Myers, Selma G, Team Building for Diverse Work
Groups, Richard Chang and Associates, Irvine, CA,
1996.

O'Mara, Julie, 101 Actions You Can Take to Value
and Mange Diversity, O'Mara and Associates, Castro
Valley, CA, 1999.

Orey, Maureen C., Successful Staffing in a Diverse
Workplace, Richard Chang and Associates, Inc., Irvine,
CA 1996.

Chapter Seven:
Working Together
Productively

Introduction

There is no question that working together
productively, regardless of race, gender, age, etc. is
critical to the strategic performance of an organization.
Organizational performance depends on workforce
members being able to effectively utilize their talents in
a cohesive way that meets the business goals and
objectives of the organization. As a manager, your role
is to help create an environment where people are able
to do their best. Since "people are the organization", it
is essential that you address the key elements that drive
productivity. These elements include but are not limited
to "expectations", "feedback", "consequences

(incentives and sanctions)", and "performer skill, knowledge and required resources."

From a diversity perspective, diverse work group members will have expectations that are imbedded in their cultural backgrounds. Some may have assumptions and beliefs that to be effective, leaders and co-workers must be directive and have a strong presence whereas others are accustomed to, and expect, a collaborative, consensus-building environment. To effectively build your diversity management capability, you need to find out what assumptions and beliefs are operating within your workforce. Each team member's background and perspective is the starting point of how opinions of what its like to work in this environment as a person who is different are formed. Their assumptions and beliefs will influence how well they will work with and communicate with members of the organization. To help assess your team's expectations, the following worksheet can be used as an exercise during a staff

The Executive's Pocket Coach to Diversity and
Inclusion Management

meeting to improve workforce productivity and
performance.

Your Views	Work force Views	Comparison between Your Views and the Workforce Views	
		Similarities	Differ-ences
My preferred meeting type is	My diverse workgroup's preferred meeting type is:		
My preferred communica tion style is:	The preferred communicat ion style of the work group given its diverse		

Your Views	Work force Views	Comparison between Your Views and the Workforce Views	
		Similarities	Differ- ences
	make up is:		
To what extent am I open and accepting of people who are different from me?	To what extent is my workgroup open and accepting are differences in each other?		
To what extent am I committed to the full	To what extent has my workgroup		

Your Views	Work force Views	Comparison between Your Views and the Workforce Views	
		Similarities	Differences
utilization of our diverse workgroup talent?	fully utilized the talents of each diverse workgroup member?		
The primary ingredient that will make us successful as a diverse work team is:	The team's view of the primary ingredient that will make us successful as a diverse work team is:		

Another critical component for working together productively is managing cultural communications barriers. Linguists estimate that the 500 words used most often in the English language can produce over 14,000 meanings. And to make matters worse, those words will generally have meaning based upon the direct relationship to a person's personal background and cultural experiences. Depending upon the degree of dissimilarity of the sender and the receiver's backgrounds, they will have more or less trouble understanding each other. As a person managing your diverse workforce, you must be skilled in understanding "why" this occurs and "how to help."

For nearly all of us, our opinions matter. So when disagreements occur with others, it can leave us feeling attacked and vulnerable and in turn, cause us to become defensive and protective of our own point of view. On the receiving end, if we are not listening carefully, we may not actually hear what the other person is saying and react to the behavior we perceive as "being in disagreement". This of course naturally frustrates and disappoints the speaker, and we may interpret that frustration as hostility and respond accordingly. In the long run, the cycle continues, the misunderstandings continue, and a poor working situation gets created.

If this poor communication continues over time, the listener and the receiver can become frustrated and begin to label the other person or themselves as inarticulate or not worth talking to for long. This sets up a pattern for bias, prejudice, and discrimination. Depending on the individual's response to this cycle, a positive or a negative environment for communication and collaborative work will arise. Let's take a look at these environmental characteristics; they often produce characteristics that are polar opposites.

Partial versus Full-bodied Listening

When we listen to someone in a full-bodied way, we not only hear the words, we pay attention to the tone

and inflection and nonverbal communication. In
essence, we capture 100% of the message. To make
certain we are really communicating, we must pay
attention to whether all three element of the sender's
message: words, tone and inflection, and nonverbal or
body language are in sync. Partial listening will cause
problems almost all of the time. At the very least,
someone in the conversation will probably walk away
feeling less valued.

Indirect versus Direct Communication

In many cultures, including our own, people rarely
verbalize what they truly mean or what they really feel.
When this happens, our communication becomes
indirect, cryptic, and puts the work team at a
disadvantage because the messages are vague, distorted,
or misinterpreted. We can vastly improve our
communication if we work with others to learn what's
needed to strengthen both the message and the

reception. In addition, it must be done in a highly respectful and sensitive way.

Neutrality versus Empathy

We reassure others when we let them know we can identify with their problems, understand their feelings, and accept their emotional reactions even when we perceive them as being excessive or even hostile to us. On the other hand, whenever we deny the legitimacy of another person's emotions, what we really do, even when we intend to be supportive, is to create a closed, hostile environment. This fosters a breeding ground for hurt feelings, ill will and potential charges of discrimination.

Superiority versus Equality

We certainly set off another person's defenses if we treat them with a sense of superiority that stems from the basis of race, gender ethnicity, wealth, intellectual ability, physical characteristics, and so on. The resultant feelings of inadequacy on the part of the listeners or their frustration causes them to hear only what their emotions are screaming at them to hear, and the subsequent resentment and hostility can be devastating to a diverse work team's performance.

Arrogant Certainty versus Flexibility to Learn

Some people have it all figured out, or at least they think so. They come across as knowing all the answers, needing no additional information, regards him or herself as the ultimate expert or authority on everything. Anyone with this style of working is highly likely to put others on the defensive and will be perceived as a source of irritation. By maintaining a flexible attitude to learn and the ability to acknowledge it by saying "I don't think that way anymore", it provides a framework for growth and high performance output.

To minimize potential misunderstandings and gaps
that can lead to conflict, here are a few tips for working
with others who are different from you:

Effective Communications Tips to Work Productively Together	
☑	**Key Ideas**
	Address communications issues head-on in an empathetic manner. Don't pretend they do not exist.
	Avoid using qualifiers that reinforce stereotypes such as "We would hire women and people of color if they had skills."
	Refrain from speaking more loudly when communicating with individuals whose English is limited. Instead, try to speak more slowly and to pronounce each syllable. But don't do so unduly, or you will inadvertently be offensive.

	Effective Communications Tips to Work Productively Together
☑	**Key Ideas**
	Use words that are gender neutral and recognize both genders e.g., salesperson versus salesman; supervisor versus foreman; etc.
	Use a wide variety of metaphors, analogies, and references, rather than just sporting or military expressions for instance.
	Be patient. It may take longer for a person whose native language is not English to process the information. Put yourself in their situation e.g., traveling to their country where you have limited or no language understanding. Would you want and need time to process what you heard to create your response?
	Use "I" messages as an assertive, culturally neutral way of saying that certain behavior is causing you difficulty but that nonetheless you respect the rights of others.

Effective Communications Tips to Work Productively Together	
☑	**Key Ideas**
	Be aware of your body language, that is, your non-verbal cues.
	Rephrase and say it again if you feel you are not being understood. Use pictures and diagrams, when appropriate. Frequently ask open-ended questions to check for the other person's understanding.
	When listening, find ways to acknowledge the speaker's emotional state. It is helpful to give them your attention and watch for cues. Don't make assumptions. Ask for clarification if you sense a perceived frustration. Check to be certain you are hearing them correctly.

Dealing with Cross-Cultural Conflict

No matter how effective you are at communicating, when working in a diverse work team, conflicts will arise. Some conflict is healthy and promotes growth, learning and understanding. The key is how you _handle_ the conflict situation. Creative sparks can flu whenever diverse ideas and perspectives "rub against one another." Many of us have been trained through our cultural programming to avoid the unpleasantness of conflict, at all costs. One of the keys to forming a diverse, high performing team will be your ability to teach both managers and team members how to view conflict in a positive light and use it constructively…"a teachable moment." Some of the potential benefits of productive conflict include the following:

Benefits of Managing Cross-Cultural and Cross-Difference Conflict	
☑	**Key Ideas**
	It creates a heightened sense of awareness of the problems that exist, and the approaches needed or used to solve them.
	Gets people to consciously consider problems and novel solutions, rather than to just allow these problems to percolate away beneath the surface.
	Promotes a greater awareness of the "isms" of discrimination and creates a determination to eliminate them (if the team has been effectively trained to do this).
	Creates a heightened sensitivity toward the needs, styles, values, frustrations, and resentment of others.
	Generates an open expression of opposing views to critique old reasoning processes and develop new decision-making tools.

Benefits of Managing Cross-Cultural and Cross-Difference Conflict	
☑	**Key Ideas**
	Energizes people to use their root cause analysis skills to openly get to the heart of the matter.
	Help the team take responsibility to be accountable to each other and improve morale.
	Helps to motivate members to come up with and articulate new solutions. Fosters creative risk-taking skills.
	Decreases costs by increasing efficiency to address problems in a direct, timely fashion.
	Improves customer relations and market penetration by addressing real needs and concerns.
	Reduces the organization's potential legal exposure.

When conflict does arise, it can be debilitating if it is not handled correctly. If your diverse work team is to work together productively, it will require a well-heeled process of communication, trust and respect among team members. These situations can get even more complicated when the team has a broad mix of people who have different first languages. The solution requires that all members of the team have both self – awareness and cultural awareness. Anytime diversity is added to a team, it changes the dynamics of the group. Through self-assessment and team analysis, you and your diverse work team can identify where cultural and other barriers can impair a team's performance and build strategies to work productively together.

References

Fernandez, John P, "Race, Gender & Rhetoric", McGraw-Hill, New York, 1999.

Hubbard, Edward E., "Techniques for Managing a Diverse Workforce", Global Insights Publishing, Petaluma, CA, 2002.

Myers, Selma G, Team Building for Diverse Work
Groups, Richard Chang and Associates, Irvine, CA,
1996.

Chapter Eight: Diversity and Organizational Change

Introduction

Effectively managing diversity requires that you are an effective manager of change. After all, diversity is not a program, "it is a process of systemic organizational change." When people think of diversity as a program, they may think that at some point they will be finished with it and can go on to something else. However, this is not the case. Generally speaking, the need to successfully manage diversity will always be a priority whenever you have people in the organization who are different in a variety of ways.

Like any other change initiative in the organization, to achieve results, your efforts to manage diversity in your workforce will require the basics of building a strategy, creating a tactical plan, taking ownership, being accountable, and implementing and measuring progress against the plan. It must also embody the principle of continuous improvement to seek new ways to create a high performing work environment utilizing diversity.

Building a Change Strategy for Diversity Management

Developing a strategy and putting a plan in place are the first steps in any change effort. What separate an ordinary manager from a great manager of diversity is their ability not only to plan, but their ability to *execute* the plan, measure progress, make adjustment, and achieve results. Without these actions, even the best plans for change can fail.

To begin mentioned in this guidebook for diversity management.

Creating a Tactical Diversity Management Plan for Change

Once your diversity management strategy is in place, it is time to consider what's needed to create a set of tactical plans to put your diversity process into action. Initiating, changing, refocusing or revitalizing your organization's commitment to create a diverse and inclusive environment starts with building a baseline. That is, building a solid understanding of the organization's current level of effectiveness in mastering the basics that influence its ability to lead and accelerate the diversity change process. This requires that you help the organization do the following:

- Analyze its communications strategy and messages

- Find out the state of the organization from the
  line perspective
- Create measures and key performance
  indicators that provide feedback proactively,
  not reactively
- Analyze and evaluate all supporting
  organizational processes and practices
- Search for "low hanging fruit as well as set a
  plan for the long-term

Analyze Its Communications Strategy And Messages

Communicate, communicate, communicate. It is
critical that the messages regarding diversity get out to
the workforce. Therefore, it is vital to determine how
effectively you are communicating. Take the time to
find out. Like any kind of change effort, a shift to a
more diverse, inclusive work environment requires the
leadership team to communicate the key themes of

diversity consistently and often if it is to become a reality. Messages that are reflected in all the dimensions and language channels, which include words, behavior and action. People within the organization must link diversity to the critical operating needs of the organization. This won't happen using a pile of slides in a PowerPoint presentation or a slick model or card that states the organization's commitment to diversity. You, as a leader, must put your own signature on key diversity themes in "one-on-one" conversations, large and small group presentations, and being visibly present to demonstrate your support. You should craft three or four themes that represent the key diversity messages you want to convey to your staff and others. What would you want to say to others that represent your values and commitment to create a diverse and inclusive organization?

Key Diversity Themes I Support:

Theme 1:

_____

_____

_____

What Makes Theme 1 Important to Me and/or the Organization?

_____

_____

_____

Messages I will Deliver About this Theme Include:

_____

_____

_____

Theme 2:

_____

_____

_____

What Makes Theme 2 Important to Me and/or the Organization?

_____

_____

_____

Messages I will Deliver About this Theme Include:

_____

_____

_____

Theme 3:

_____

_____

_____

What Makes Theme 3 Important to Me and/or the Organization?

_____

_____

_____

Messages I will Deliver About this Theme Include:

_____

_____

_____

Theme 4:

_____

_____

_____

What Makes Theme 4 Important to Me and/or the Organization?

_____

_____

_____

Messages I will Deliver About this Theme Include:

_____

_____

_____

Take the time to schedule when you will implement your diversity communications plan delivering your key diversity messages (at the next staff meeting, in a one-on-one conversation, during the next Town Hall meeting with your department or the organization). Think about the leader and speakers that have had the most influence on you hearing their message. What did they do to capture your attention and make the message stand out in your mind? Think about the fact that your audience will be made of a diverse group of people and about the most effective way to communicate such that they are receptive.

In addition, be authentic. Your staff has heard you talk about things before and have judged you by it. If you have not been supportive of diversity previously, let them know what things led you to your current position and what they can count on you for in the future. Remember, everyone has the capacity to change if they really want to. You do not have to talk about what you did not do in the past. The past, including the good and the challenging, helped you to get to the point where you are today. And that includes gaining new knowledge about diversity and learning from it. Your messages must be delivered convincingly, consistently and often, and you must be visibly supportive to effect change.

Find Out The State Of The Organization From The Line Perspective

Creating a diverse organization with equal access at all levels and an environment that respects, values and engages the talents of all its people does not happen or maintain itself automatically. It requires an ongoing strategic focus with systems, processes, values and people to support it. Like any other change process, it takes time, conviction, and personal involvement. As a change agent and leader, you must get personally involved to ask: "What's happening in our organization that supports diversity? What's not happening? What should I be doing right now to influence action towards our diversity vision? Towards the messages I support?

By taking time to assess where you are in the process, you open yourself up for the broader opportunities that may be available. You must model the inclusion process by getting others at all levels involved and working together productively towards the diversity vision.

Create Measures And Key Performance Indicators That Provide Feedback Proactively, Not Reactively

Compliance with laws and governmental regulations is a small portion of what diversity is about. Diversity encompasses much, much more. Effective diversity performance and change is driven by execution, not by strategy alone and diversity measurement drives execution.

It is a known fact that the best leaders accomplish their strategy by having goals and excellent feedback mechanisms to know they are making progress. They make it a point to personally inspect and find out how things are going. They use tools such as surveys, focus groups, Town Hall meetings, consultants, steering committees and the like to stay informed of the diversity change management process. They conduct informal reviews and check for problems. They create diversity metrics that are linked to the organization's strategy such that they know if the workforce is being fully utilized.

By working proactively instead of reactively, they are able to address issues before they become major problems. People respond to what is measured and reviewed. It helps to keep the diversity change effort focused and promotes continuous improvement.

Analyze and Evaluate All Supporting Organizational Processes And Practices

An effective diversity manager in a change process will search for leverage points. That is, they look for influence points in other processes that help integrate diversity and inclusion into the organization's mainstream. They assess options and opportunities to enhance current organizational processes so they include diversity supportive language, processes and methods. This search for processes covers the gamut from operational processes and performance planning to work-life, customer strategies and supply-chain management. Subtle messages and more overt processes for diversity and inclusion are a key part of the fabric that covers the way an organization does business.

Search For "Low Hanging Fruit As Well As Set A Plan For The Long-Term

In addition to a longer-term, strategic approach, it is also important to spend some time to consciously look for and recognize the things that are going well in the organization. Often, during your informal review, you will find people or diverse work teams doing outstanding work. Or, you may find opportunities for integrating diversity into the day-to-day process with little effort. Make it a point to seize these opportunities and recognize those who are making diversity happen in the organization.

In addition, spend some time consciously looking for areas that can be improved. Watch out for situations where the employee base may be receiving poor or mixed messages about the organization's commitment to diversity. Be sure to let employees know about your point of view and the key messages that are a part of

your personal commitment. Leadership teams that talk
favorably about diversity and building an inclusive
work environment in public, yet they make few efforts
to be inclusive in their own interactions with other (or
people outside their inner circle) are suspect. Here are a
couple of contradictory diversity management practices
to watch out for...

- Staff who talk about being friendly and
  welcoming to anyone, yet they are
  unapproachable and grumpy.
- Managers who repeatedly cancel appointment
  or are late or take calls when dealing with
  people who are different from themselves, yet
  this does not happen with their "inner circle"
  group.
- Managers who consistently schedule meetings
  with Sunday travel.
- Managers espousing the value of diversity of
  thought and style, but who are quick to stamp
  out any new idea.

What examples come to mind for you?

It is critical to remember that your strategies, measures, and messages are the basic fundamentals of change. It is up to you to plan your diversity change work and then work your plan!

References

Hubbard, Edward E., "Techniques for Managing a Diverse Workforce", Global Insights Publishing, Petaluma, CA, 2002.

Chapter Nine:
Management Action Plan

Introduction

Effectively managing diversity requires commitment, planning, feedback and accountability. It is critical that you develop a personal action plan to put what you have learned into action. Managing diversity successfully takes both awareness and action. But the action you take may vary according to the differences in your workplace. For example, cultural differences may require understanding and communication, while gender pay differential issues may require policy changes that must be implemented. The specific actions you take will depend on the issues, the expected outcome, your organization's need, the impact on your workforce, and above all, your commitment to diversity.

How Can You Improve?

Research and first-hand observation has taught us that diversity management competencies can be developed. If you really want to develop competency to improve your ability to manage diversity, the tools, information, and techniques in this pocket guide along with the following steps will get you off to a good start:

1. **Understand Yourself.** Take a look at your scores on the Managing Diversity Profile. Compare your current level with where you would like to be.

2. **Understand the Competency.** Study the behaviors and processes mentioned in this Manager's Pocket Guide to Diversity Management. Make sure you understand what each competency area means, and identify the ways you could demonstrate the various behaviors.

3. **Practice the Competency.** Focus on one
    competency area or two, at the most. Plan to
    use those behaviors as often as possible. Spend
    time deciding how you can use them. Start
    with behavioral changes that begin to stretch
    your thinking and work towards more
    challenging behaviors. The first time you try
    some of the behavioral changes, you may not
    succeed. It may also seem a little awkward.
    That's OK. Give yourself permission to fail
    once or twice.

4. **Get Feedback.** You may not always be the
    best judge of your own diversity management
    competencies. Ask someone else to help you.
    Make it clear to the other person what you are
    trying to accomplish, and ask him or her to
    give you feedback on your progress. Or, ask
    them and others to assess your skill level by
    taking the 360° version of the Managing
    Diversity Profile (the Diversity Leadership
    Competency Profile). Alternatively, try to find

a hard measure of your success, one that does not rely on your opinion. This step leads back to step 1 – understanding where you are now.

This guide is packed with diversity management information and several tools you can use. As you get more practice, your command of the diversity competency will improve – as long as you continue to get objective feedback on your performance to know where you stand. Some of the diversity management competencies are more challenging than others and may take much more time. Be sure to set realistic goals for yourself in terms of how quickly you will start to own the new behaviors and start to see change.

Below, is an action planning form. Complete the form for each competency area in which you would like to improve. The form asks you to make decisions about:

- **Diversity/Inclusion Management Competency** (which Diversity/Inclusion

Management Competency area you want to
work on).

- **Your Improvement Goal** (the specific
  improvement objective you want to
  accomplish)
- **Measures of Success** (the evidence that will
  indicate you've succeeded)
- **Completion Dates** (the dates by which you
  will have competed the action items and
  achieved your goal)
- **Support** (someone to whom you can turn for
  coaching, advice, and encouragement. It is
  also an opportunity to get feedback from
  others who are different from yourself)

The Executive's Pocket Coach to Diversity and Inclusion Management

Strategic Diversity and Inclusion Action Plan

Diversity & Inclusion Management Competency	Your Improvement Goal	Action Items	Measures of Success	Completion Dates	Support

Measuring Progress

There is an old saying that "you can't manage what you don't measure". Therefore, it is critical that you periodically measure your progress against the plan you create. During the process of individual and organizational change, it can be tempting to revert back to old habits and ways. Your old cultural programming software can creep back in and re-runs of old behavior try to take over again.

It is crucial that you set up reinforcement processes and new patterns that take shape as current operating norms. Make it a point to meet with employees and ask: "How are we doing as a diverse work team?," "If I could do one thing differently to make me even more effect as a diverse work team manager, what would you suggest I do?", "What is one thing that the organization can do differently to improve its diversity efforts overall?

Get people together. Celebrate achievements with them. Develop a theme or focus based on the needs of your organization. At best, you will want to create an agenda that leads to an uplifting conclusion. Use that time as a forum to talk about specific challenges. Keep it positive by listening and acknowledging issues. Also engaging people in seeing their role in participating in resolving key cross-cultural interaction and other issues. It is important to let your team paint the picture of what diversity and inclusion will be like from their unique perspective and how it will contribute to making the organization better.

Walking the Talk

It takes a great deal of courage to understand, accept, and own up to your competency in managing diversity. It is easy to give up when things get tough or when it appears that "diversity" is no longer in vogue. It is easy to point fingers at others when the organization is not as welcoming to diversity as we would like it to be. Nonetheless, when we point fingers, at least three of our fingers point back. It is critical that you "walk your own talk." A lot will depend on what you do personally.

It is important to become conscious of what your own filters and personal biases are. You have to confront them and make certain you fully utilize the true gifts that your diverse workforce brings to the table. You can say all you want about your beliefs in diversity and inclusion, but if you don't take actions to prove it, people won't believe you.

Walking the talk means that you make certain you are living the diversity values standard you want or are holding others to meet. When you lead by example, employees get the message loud and clear that you not only talk about the importance of diversity, you live it by the way you interact with others. Modeling diversity leadership is critical for improved performance using diversity. Remember, the net effect and impact of your

behavior is multiplied over the number of lives you
touch as a manager. You play a vital role in whether
diversity in your organization is a reality or myth. I
hope that you will choose to be the "difference that
helps makes the diversity difference!"

Chapter Ten: Creating an Effective Diversity and Inclusion Communications Strategy

Building a Communications Strategy

A Diversity and Inclusion communications strategy involves a multifaceted plan that keeps members of the organization informed about the Diversity and Inclusion process. In general, the objectives of this strategy are to: broadcast the strategic business rationale for utilizing diversity and inclusion, build and maintain support, involve the whole organizational system, and provide continuous feedback and ongoing communication about what is happening and why. The design of such a strategic process should begin by answering several fundamental questions:

- What are the objectives of the communication strategy?

- Who are the target audiences?

- What is the key message for each audience?

- What are the appropriate metrics to analyze the impact of the

communication per its objectives?

- What is the appropriate media for each audience?

- What is the timeframe for each stage of the communication strategy?

- How will we know that the communication has been received?

In thinking through a communication and metrics strategy, it is usually helpful to consider the organization's political climate by asking questions:

- What are we trying to achieve at this point?

- Who do we need to involve for the metrics to be accepted?

- Who needs to know what and when?

- Who are the "gatekeepers" who could block or support the communications message and/or its metrics?

- How able is a particular person or group to really "hear" what is being said?

- How can we communicate the leadership team's commitment to the diversity change process?

A key first step in any diversity communications strategy is to highlight the business rationale and benefits to the organization for moving in this direction. The challenge is to communicate frequently at the beginning of the initiative to assure people of the leadership team's commitment and support. This can be done through channels such as newsletters, regular meetings, management retreats, staff meetings, town hall meetings and the like. Communications initiatives set the tone so people understand the overall effort and the rationale behind it. As a result, when employees are asked to participate (e.g., through task force involvement, focus groups, surveys, celebrations, affinity groups, etc.), they will understand how

important their involvement is and how it will be linked
to the overall effort.

Defining your Diversity
Communications Metrics Strategy

Defining diversity communications metrics usually
requires at least three distinct steps. In three steps, you
can translate your communication messages or
strategies into specific performance indicators.

First, it requires that you identify specific diversity
communications objectives linked to the overall
business strategy and what is needed to accomplish
each objective. Second, you have to determine the
critical success factors, e.g, inform, evoke an action,
etc. Third, consider each critical success factor area and
define key diversity performance metrics or indicators
that will track that area's success.

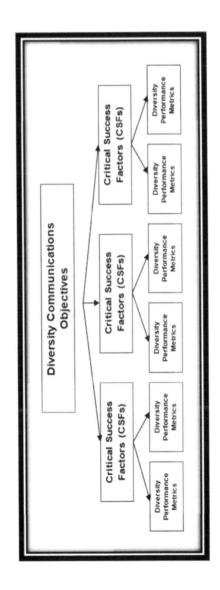

Let's examine each stage of the process in more detail.

Identifying Specific Diversity Communication Objectives

Creating effective diversity communications metrics begins with identifying specific diversity communications objectives that are aligned with the organizational diversity strategy. These objectives focus on the accomplishment of an outcome related to the diversity strategy, such as showcasing the use of diverse work teams to generate new, innovative target market segment products and services. In addition, these metrics must help sort out whether the message accomplished its intent. This intent may include the need to:

- **Inform** — Did the target audience learn something they didn't know about diversity as a result of the message?

- **Instill an Attitude** — Did the target audience adopt a certain feeling about the diversity process and/or its initiatives as a result of the message?

- **Generate an Action** — Did the target audience do something diversity-related as a result of the message?

Once you know your objectives, write them down and check to see if they are 1) specific, 2) measurable, and 3) realistic. If they are specific, they will be phrased in concrete, active words such as "analyze," "recognize," "recall," "state," "explain," "summarize," "select," etc. If your objectives are not specific, you must come down the abstraction ladder until they are. For example, if the intent is to "generate" an action, does your objective start with a word that is behaviorally specific, that is, does it state an action you can observe someone doing? Even if your objectives

The Executive's Pocket Coach to Diversity and
Inclusion Management

are specific, they may not be measurable. For example, you may want an audience to "feel good or better," but how will you measure what "good or better" looks like? In other words, how will you know that you achieved your message outcome? Can you ask for a vote or get immediate oral or written feedback from the audience? Look for ways to identify and isolate the root change your diversity communication intends and measure that change as part of the strategy.

The third criterion is equally important: Are these objectives realistic? Have you bit off more than you can chew? For example, can you realistically expect to lay out the entire diversity strategy, its initiatives and importance to the organization's business strategy in a 15-minute presentation at the next town hall meeting? If your reply is no, it is time to redefine your objectives, limiting them to what can realistically be accomplished.

You must also draw on what you have learned about your audience. What can you reasonably hope to

Page 340

accomplish with this group of people? If you need them to make a decision about some key element of the diversity process and they are not decision makers, can you really expect the communications metrics to credibly show that the diversity strategy was advanced by this message? It might be better to set objectives that would give this audience information about the diversity process enlisting their support such that they, in turn, are equipped to influence the real-decision makers.

These are just a few considerations. A sample list of diversity communication objectives may include the following:

- Communicate leadership commitment to diversity

- Communicate the business rationale and benefits of diversity

- Communicate the benefits of diversity to the local community

- Keep communications channels open among all employee groups

- Celebrate and acknowledge the importance of the contributions of all employees

- Communicate why diversity efforts are critical to the current and future success of the organization

- Demonstrate the use of strategic diversity management approaches and their impact on improving organizational climate

- Using the previous three monthly issues of the company newsletter, employees will "recall" two feature stories about the organization's diversity process.

- Etc.

Determining Your Critical Success Factor Areas

A *critical success factor* (CSF) area is an important "must-achieve," "make-or-break" performance category for the diversity message. They typically focus on the intended outcome for success in that area. In general, a

sample set of critical success factor areas might include
outcomes such as:

- Generating open communication channels
among all employee groups

- Identifying leadership commitment to diversity

- Creating the business rationale and benefits of
diversity

- Determining the benefits of diversity to the
local community

- Recognizing the contributions of all
employees

- Identifying the diversity efforts that are critical
to current and future organizational success

- Improving organizational climate for diversity

- Showcasing diversity progress

Identifying and Utilizing Key Diversity Communications Metrics

Diversity performance measures are the tools we use to determine whether we are meeting our objectives and moving toward the successful implementation of our communications strategy. Specifically, we may describe diversity performance measures as quantifiable (normally, but not always) standards used to evaluate and communicate performance against expected results. However, no simple definition can truly capture the power that well-crafted and well-communicated performance measures can have on an organization.

Measures communicate value creation in ways that even the most charismatic CEO's speeches never can. They function as a tool to drive desired action, provide all employees with direction in how they can help contribute to the organization's overall diversity goals, and supply management with a tool in determining overall progress toward the diversity vision. So performance measures are critically important to your diversity communications strategy, however, generating effective diversity communications performance measures may not be as simple as you think.

Measurement is defined as the assignment of numbers to properties (or characteristics) of objects based on a set of rules. Because we are often interested in the quantities related to a diversity outcome, numerical representation is important; however, we are not interested in just any quantities — we want the quantities to have meaning. For example, if we conduct a diverse workforce communications survey and ask the question: "Do managers/supervisors keep employees informed regarding the organization's diversity efforts?" Knowing that the average score is 3.5 on a five-point scale does not have much inherent meaning. Is scoring 3.5 good or bad? Or consider an employee turnover rate of 15 percent. Percentage points have more inherent meaning than five-point scales, but simply observing the number does not reveal much about whether 15 percent is a problem or not.

To add meaning to these levels, we need to add context and a baseline. This is the appeal of a benchmark. If we find that our 3.5 on a five-point scale is considerably better than our industry peers' ratings on the same exact question, we can begin to attach some significance to that measure. However, we might observe that our 3.5 is considerably below our internal historical level on this measure. Whether we discover we are doing better than our peers or not maintaining our internal historical performance, in both cases we have made interpretations about the relative value only (e.g., we are better or worse than some standard).

In neither case do we have any measure of strategic value. In other words, what difference does it make whether we have a 3.0 or 4.0 value on a five-point diverse workforce communications survey? To have strategic value, the measure must be expressed in numerical units that offer inherent performance significance (such as a percentage of management commitment to diversity, benefit of diversity to improved market share, increased retention of women and people of color beyond the three-year mark, etc.). In other words, we have to translate the measure into performance-relevant units.

In a recent study by the American Institute of Certified Public Accountants, 27 percent of respondents stated "the ability to define and agree upon measures" as the most frequent barrier to implementing or revising a performance measurement system. This statement highlights the importance of gaining agreement to the overall communications strategy, its objectives, and its critical success factors prior to selecting appropriate

measures. Perfecting your diversity performance
metrics will present you with numerous questions and
issues, such as:

- How many measures should you have?
- How often should you measure?
- What about shared accountabilities?
- Could your measures be contaminated?
- Are your measures reliable?
- Which performance comparatives are best?
- Is there a balance of "Lead" and "Lag"
measures?
- Should you combine measures into an index?
- Is denominator management a risk?
- How can good measures be made better?

Whether this is the first time you have thought
about diversity communications performance measures
or you are well experienced in tracking overall diversity

communications performance, you will be challenged by these issues.

To help you get started on your communications metrics journey, here's a list of potential measures:

- Number of diversity-related press releases sent to major news outlets
- Number of diversity-related press releases sent to secondary news outlets
- Number of diversity-related speeches delivered at key internal functions
- Number of diversity-related speeches delivered at key community functions
- Percent of media spent on demographic groups
- Percent of creative advertisements (print, TV) featuring people by demographic group (African Americans, Asians, Hispanics, Women, etc.)
- Percent of photo diversity with officers and without officers appearing in your annual report

- Number of diversity-related photos of company employees appearing at community events and in programs or brochures

- Year-to-date Communications Department funds spent on sponsorships of community and diversity-related events

- Number of diversity-related publications produced (brochures, reports)

- Content analysis of corporate website for diversity-related content

- Lead story — percent of top 10 news outlets

- Supporting stories — percent of top 10 news outlets

- Number of diversity ads by demographic group that generated sales of $1,000 or more

- Number of diversity ads cited by women and people of color which informed them of the organization's commitment to diversity.

Each of the sample measures shown above are designed to give feedback on achieving the intent to "inform," "instill an attitude," or "generate an action" related to a specific diversity-focused communication. Diversity communication metrics not only inform organizational audiences that long-term diversity strategies are in place to achieve competitive success, but also provide an important basis for feedback and accountability.

Summary

Measuring the effectiveness of your diversity communications is a mandatory prerequisite for diversity performance and success. These metrics and their accompanying strategy help set the stage and model requirements that drive, direct and select methods to keep all key stakeholders informed

regarding the progress of the diversity change process
and its value to the organization.

Remember, as you move through your diversity
and inclusion change process, apply measurable
communication processes and share diversity initiative
feedback. Having a solid base of support and
commitment from leadership, an effective
communications strategy and strategically effective
communications metrics enables the organization to
successfully manage critical diversity challenges and
achieve its vision for the future.

About the Author

Dr. Edward E. Hubbard, Ph.D.

Dr. Edward E. Hubbard is President and CEO of Hubbard & Hubbard, Inc., Petaluma, CA, an international organization and human performance-consulting corporation that specializes in techniques for applied business performance improvement, Diversity Return on Investment (DROI®) measurement and analytics, instructional design and strategic organizational development. He is the author of more than 40 books.

Dr. Hubbard was an honoree at the Inaugural International Society of Diversity and Inclusion Professionals Legends of Diversity Ceremony in Rio Grande, Puerto Rico where he received the "**Legends of Diversity Award**" for establishing the "Diversity ROI Analytics" and "Diversity Measurement Fields/Disciplines". Dr. Hubbard received the "**Excellence in Global Leadership Award**" from the

World HRD Congress as Pioneer and Founder of the
Diversity ROI Analytics and Measurement fields. The
highest individual professional award given.

The American Society for Training and
Development (ASTD) inducted Dr. Ed Hubbard into
the prestigious "ASTD New Guard for 2003". The
July/August 2007 Issue of Profiles in Diversity Journal
featured Dr. Hubbard as the "Diversity Pioneer" in
Diversity Measurement. Dr. Hubbard serves on the
Harvard Business Review, Diversity Executive
Magazine and Strategic Diversity & Inclusion
Management (SDIM) magazine Editorial Advisory
Boards.

Dr. Hubbard served as Director, Developmental
Education and Assistant Professor, The Ohio State
University. A sample of Dr. Hubbard's corporate
experience includes Programming Analyst and
Manager, Battelle Memorial Institute, Systems Analyst,
Informatics Corporation, Systems Engineer, Xerox
Corporation, Organization Development and Education
Specialist, Mead Corporation, Director of Training,
Organizational Development, Communications and

Compensation for the 17 Billion Dollar McKesson Corporation.

Dr. Hubbard is an expert in Organizational Behavior, Organizational Analysis, Applied Performance Improvement and ROI Measurement Strategies, Strategic Planning, Diversity Measurement and Analytics, and Strategic Organizational Change Methodologies. He holds a Practitioner Certification and Master Practitioner Certification in Neurolinguistic Programming (NLP), a Neuro-science discipline. Dr. Hubbard earned Bachelors, Masters Degrees and earned a Ph.D. with Honors in Business Administration.

1.5 Minute YouTube Introduction of Dr. Hubbard and His Diversity and Inclusion Return on Investment (DROI®) Measurement Work can be seen by using the link below:

http://www.youtube.com/watch?v=ZoVqbM9wty8

Some of Dr. Hubbard's books include the following:

Other books include "Measuring the ROI Impact of Employee Resource Groups (ERGs)and Business Resource Groups (BRGs): Ensuring Employee Resource Group Initiatives Drive Business and Organizational Results co-authored with Dr. Myra K. Hubbard, co-Founder of Hubbard & Hubbard, Inc. and "Diversity ROI Fundamentals: Ensuring Diversity Initiatives Demonstrate ROI Impact Value on the Bottom-line".

His most recent book includes "Mastering Secrets
of Personal Success: Tools to Create the Life You Want
which is used for personal and employee self-
empowerment training and skill-building.

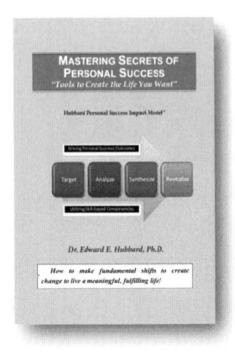

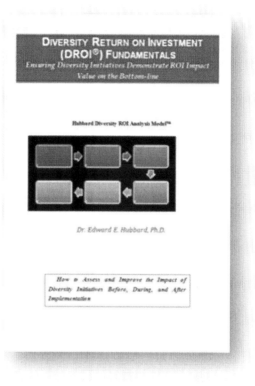

MEASURING THE ROI IMPACT OF ERGs AND BRGs
Ensuring Employee Resource Group Initiatives Drive Business and Organizational Results

Hubbard ERG/BRG ROI Analysis Model™

Dr. Edward E. Hubbard, Ph.D.

Dr. Myra K. Hubbard, Ph.D.

How to Assess and Improve Employee Resource Group and Business Resource Group Initiatives Before, During, and After Implementation

About the Hubbard Diversity
Measurement and Productivity Institute

"Creating Applied Sciences for Measuring Diversity Performance & Results"

Hubbard & Hubbard, Inc. has established the Hubbard Measurement & Productivity Institute (DM&P) to provide measurement skills, certification workshop and applied learning conferences for assessing, measuring and evaluating diversity results in organizations.

Based on the ground-breaking book: "Measuring Diversity Results" by Dr. Edward E. Hubbard, this institute is dedicated to assisting practitioners and other professionals with tools and techniques to research and develop measurable diversity business processes as well as case examples for diversity which clearly demonstrate impact on the financial bottom-line of the

organization. Our mission is to provide the most up-to-
date tools diversity professionals need to make
effective, timely decisions to create a measurable
performance impact! Sample workshop titles include:

- Measuring Diversity Results
- Building a Measurable Diversity Strategic
  Plan
- How to Calculate Diversity Return-on-
  Investment
- Building A Diversity Measurement Scorecard
- Creating and Implementing a Diversity
  Culture and Systems Audit
- How to Construct a Diversity Business Case
- Conducting a Cultural Due Diligence Audit
- Measuring Supplier Diversity Utilization
- Assessing Diversity Training Impact
- Creating Measures for Diverse Work Team
  Productivity
- Measuring Diversity Results: An Executive
  Overview

In addition, the Diversity Measurement and
Productivity Institute (DM&P) offer a wide range of
diversity productivity workshops for employees,
managers and executives such as:

- Diversity in the Workplace
- Diversity Leadership Skills
- Communicating Across Cultures
- Supervising a Diverse Workforce
- Diversity Leadership Skills for Executives
- Etc.

Online and other Products available through the
Diversity Measurement and Productivity Institute
(DM&P) to support your diversity management skills
include:

- Diversity Leadership Competency Profile –
  Full 360° version
- The Diversity Baseline Audit
- The Diversity 9-S Framework Audit
- Managing Expectations Survey
- The Diversity Climate Analysis
- MDR Stat Pak 1 Software: Diversity
  Measurement Scorecard Startup Metrics
- MDR Stat Pak 3 Software: Measuring
  Diversity Staffing and Recruitment Impact
- Metriclink® Online Dashboard and Scorecard
- Metriclink® Online Talent Management
  PowerBoard™ Dashboard Tracking service
- Etc.

The Diversity Measurement and Productivity Institute (DM&P) also offers a full range of Diversity Certification Courses that result in two primary certifications for internal practitioners:

- Certified Internal Diversity Trainer
- Certified Internal Diversity Advisor

Please visit our website at www.HubbardNHubbardInc.com for more information and schedules. Hubbard & Hubbard, Inc. has a broad range of services to meet your needs:

Index